Nantucket Journeys

Nantucket Journeys

Exploring the Island,
Its Architecture,
And Its Past

Catherine A. Garland

Down East Books

Photographs Are by the Author.

Illustrations Are by the Author, with Assistance from Catherine Cunningham, AIA

Copyright © 1988 by Catherine Ann Garland
ISBN 0-89272-247-9
Library of Congress Catalog Card Number 88-70746
Design by Edith Allard
Printed at Kingsport Press, Kingsport, Tenn.

5 4 3 2 1

Down East Books / Camden, Maine 04843

For My Mother and Father

Contents

In the Neighborhoods

Foreword

By Edouard A. Stackpole

◼The island of Nantucket boasts mainly of the town of Nantucket, and much of *Nantucket Journeys* deals with this "town in the sea." The story of Nantucket Town is the story of a people who were reared in the sea, who adopted the sea for a means of livelihood and developed a world-famous whaling industry. The coming of the Quaker religion brought to the island a long period of community life unlike that of the nearby mainland settlements. Coupled with the steady progress of the whale fishery, this gave Nantucket a unique position as virtually an independent kingdom in the sea.

To her study of Nantucket's environment and architectural development, Catherine Garland has brought some of the vigor and determination of those early Nantucketers. She has dealt wisely with the town's early growth and touched upon the relative wisdom of the first builders.

The preservation of the old town, despite the problems of depression, a great fire, and economic disaster, brought a new era— the discovery of Nantucket as a resort town for people who sought something different. During the development of the summer business, the town was able to protect its historic atmosphere, and Miss Garland pays tribute to those days of change as well. Fortunately, people who came here to summer made their holdings a part of the tradition of age, and thus preserved the appearance of Nantucket Town.

Miss Garland is well aware of the gradual development that led to the town we have today. It is a place both touched by the past and blessed by the concern of today's townspeople; concerted action brought about a passage of the historic districts act of 1956, which has protected Nantucket's character.

Nantucket Journeys will also alert its readers to some of the problems that face the modern, growing Nantucket. This introduction to the architectural lines of the old homes, the original layouts of the old streets, and the special quality of the whole town, brings an awareness of the necessity of preserving Nantucket's special history. As Catherine Garland points out, this is a place that deserves to be better understood, and in her book she gives us an opportunity to do that.

Guyl—
Thanks for
all your help and
patience
Best Wishes
[signature]

Acknowledgments

This book was a bicoastal production, for people on two coasts were involved in the creation of it. I would first like to thank the resident experts on the East Coast. Edouard Stackpole provided many intriguing conversations and patiently reviewed the text. His contributions and insight have been invaluable. The staff and administration of the Nantucket Historical Association at the Peter Foulger Museum helped to find maps and documents, and allowed me working space while on the Island. Specifically, I would like to thank John Welch, Jacqueline Haring, Gayl Michael, and Virginia Newhouse. Patricia Butler, Executive Secretary for the Nantucket Historic District Commission, and James Lentkowski, Director of the Nantucket Conservation Foundation, both graciously supplied needed information. In addition, Lucille Sanguinetti and the people at the Nantucket Saltmarsh kindly shared their Nantucket experiences with me.

I would also like to acknowledge my local experts on the West Coast, who left their homes in California (in September, December, or March) and came to Nantucket with me to discuss this project: my parents, whom I must thank for their help and support, not to mention that wild jeep ride out to Great Point; Darlene LaCombe, Architect, who helped coordinate the data for the journeys; Victoria Van der Kam, who proofread the text on numerous occasions and always offered constructive criticism; and Catherine Cunningham, AIA, who helped and advised on the illustrations, reviewed the text from the standpoint of another architect and educator, and offered enlightening and reassuring dialogue throughout the entire process.

Finally, I would like to thank those special students at Cal Poly, Pomona, who have had the courage to not only ask questions in class, but to question my answers as well—and you all know who you are.

Introduction

Nantucket! Take out your map and look at it. See what a real corner of the world it occupies; how it stands there, away off shore, more lonely than the Eddystone lighthouse. Look at it—a mere hillock, and elbow of sand; all beach, without a background. There is more sand there than you would use in twenty years as a substitute for blotting paper. Some gamesome wights will tell you that they have to plant weeds there, they don't grow naturally; that they import Canada thistles; that they have to send beyond seas for a spile to stop a leak in an oil cask; that pieces of wood in Nantucket are carried about like bits of the true cross in Rome; that people there plant toadstools before their houses, to get under the shade in summer time; that one blade of grass makes an oasis, three blades in a day's walk a prairie; that they wear quicksand shoes, something like Laplander snowshoes; that they are so shut up, belted about, every way inclosed, surrounded, and made an utter island of by the ocean, that to their very chairs and tables small clams will sometimes be found adhering, as to the backs of sea turtles. But these extravaganzas only show that Nantucket is no Illinois.

—Herman Melville
Moby Dick, 1851

The Nantucket of Herman Melville's day is no more; only the whaling ghosts have stayed behind to romp and play in the town and buildings built long ago. The tiny island community has evolved into a more poignant environment than even Melville could have imagined. It is infused with the same sense of meaning, though the purpose has changed with the passage of time. The little island, like a fine wood carving, has simply aged well. I first encountered Nantucket in 1982, while on my way to Rome for research, on leave from the University of California at Irvine. A colleague suggested that I stop at Nantucket on my way across the Atlantic. Having arrived at Boston's Logan airport with enough luggage to get through the Italian winter, I struggled up to the commuter airlines. "Nantucket Island," I said, and handed my ticket to the smiling man behind the counter.

"Nantucket." He whistled, emphasizing the first syllable. "Come with me."

I followed him to an airplane that was scarcely larger than a Volkswagen with wings. "It's just you and me this time of year," declared the pilot, who was the very same man that had checked my baggage. "You can sit up in the front." Then he said rather matter-of-factly, "You're just in time, we're expecting a nor'easter. Here, hold this." He tossed me a hefty leather pouch. About halfway across Cape Cod, sitting in the copilot's seat, I discovered that I was holding the mail.

That brief introduction hardly prepared me for what was to come. It was late October then, and the summer crowds had all gone home. Left behind was the bare skeleton of a resort town out of season. Nantucket was like no place that I had ever experienced. It seemed to be a town that time had graciously forgotten, and I had taken a step back at least 150 years in American history. Without the activity of summer tourism, the town was very still. I walked up and down the near-empty streets, marveling at the thought that if I were very quiet I could almost hear the click-clacking of the horses and carriages on Main Street, the belly laugh of a fat, prosperous whaling captain, the cry of a recent widow, or sense the heavy stillness of a Quaker meeting. Nantucket is a frozen moment in a dance step from the nineteenth century. It is one of those special places where you are never really alone, but always in tune with the rhythm of an era that once was.

My plane left for Rome, but I never completely forgot Nantucket. Every year since that first visit, I have returned to the island, mostly in the off-season. Sometime later, when I was asked to teach a class at the California Polytechnic State University at Pomona, on "The Meaning of Architecture," Nantucket persisted in my mind. What is the meaning of architecture? And why do we remember certain environments that we have chanced to experience, while forgetting those in which we live from day to day? These thoughts continued to intrigue me.

Perhaps it is too simplistic to say that we appreciate an interesting environment more than a boring one; nevertheless, it is true and it is a beginning. I have found that a memorable environment must be an intact area, easily understood as a natural unit, and most often unique in its character. Water appears to be important: views of water, views over water, revealing a little at a time or a panorama. Within the community there is usually a sharp awareness of the past, a sense of history and culture still apparent today, not only in the buildings but most certainly in spirit. The celebration of the process of marketing occurs naturally in the most memorable settings. It is a

Nantucket Journeys

xiv

continuation of our Old World heritage, helping to promote a strong sense of community, gathering, and sociability. In these environments, dining often becomes a ceremony, and many fine restaurants can be found.

The architecture defers to the sense of place and community, and helps to compose an active living, working environment. The aged structures, moreover, are not isolated icons of the past, roped off and separated into a nursing home for old buildings. Instead, they have been adapted for use in the present, while maintaining their dignity of the past. The buildings are allowed to speak their histories, and in so doing tell the story of the culture that built them.

The memorable environment is also a friendly one, provoking in the visitor a strong desire for discovery. It pulls at all of the senses, not just that of sight. Finally, the memorable community has an active street life, which helps to keep the community safe, so that our natural tendencies of curiosity and discovery can be carried out. Needless to say, Nantucket fits all of these criteria.

This book is intended to be a process for exploration. You might say, "Oh, but by the very nature of the word *exploration*, do I really need a formula? Or even at that, a guide?" Children do not seem to need formulas, adults do. Somewhere between childhood and adulthood many of us have lost that vital curiosity, that imagination, which only yesterday gave us the courage to build forts and tree-houses, and the innocence that believed them to be skyscrapers. Children are much more aware of their built environments simply because they are not afraid to become involved with them. This book is an invitation to come and experience physical history, hand-in-hand with the inherent child in all of us.

The process is divided into four parts. Part I concentrates on understanding the facts, or how this environment has developed: the evolution of the town, the architecture, and nature.

Part II analyzes these facts creatively: what are the elements and physical events that have resulted? Here, I will present a brief discussion on architectural elements such as color, texture, line, and form as they relate to Nantucket architecture. In addition, these elements are governed by the principles called rhythm, balance, proportion, and scale. When these concepts are combined in a harmonious way, they define neighborhoods and communities.

The third part is "the Nantucket experience." Maps, photographs, and dialogue compose walking or bicycling journeys along some of the more memorable streets and lanes on Nantucket. The journeys have been written so that you can stroll the streets and ponder the history, or sit back and reflect on the concepts presented without actually being there. Imagine standing in front of a particular scene where the cobblestones of the main street give way to the smaller, more irregular stones of a private path. Two parallel ruts have been carefully worn over time and converge in the distance upon a farm house, barely noticeable from where you stand. Just a trace of white clapboard reveals itself, but the simple pleasures of yesterday are already running through your mind. It is Indian summer. Could that extraordinary smell actually be pumpkins? The split-rail fence, too, marches along the path, quickening its rhythm to fall upon the by-now curious farmhouse. This fence, you note, was once definitive, separating landscape and path, but now the edge is blurred, yielding to nature and the passage of time. The surrounding trees have grown tall enough to form a canopy over the path, and the dappling effect produced by the sun shining through the leaves and resting softly on the cobblestones invites you to walk forward.

A bit of nostalgia, a bit of history, and a strong dose of visual delight, such is a typical Nantucket street. The deceiving simplicity of Nantucket streets reveals, upon closer scrutiny, a startling complexity that pits one human sense against another. This collision of senses, however, is exactly what pleases us.

The final part of this book, the Afterword, discusses how and why this town has been preserved. There are over eight hundred buildings on Nantucket that predate the American Civil War; the town itself was declared a National Historic Landmark in 1966. Because of a series of fortuitous events, we have an entire historic American town preserved for our enjoyment in the present. Nantucket represents our Pompeii. It asks for an active exploration. The Nantucket experience occurs over a period of time, as it is not only a visual experience, but a mental one as well. It encompasses actually being there and most especially, afterward, when we return to our own homes and communities, having taken a little bit of the island with us.

Most environments can only be appreciated by moving through them and listening to what they have to tell you. You need to walk or ride a bicycle through these special places because a walking or pedaling pace allows you to slow down and enjoy the small and overlooked. A passive explanation, or being shown or driven about Nantucket, will not provoke the same mental images as would exploring on your own. As Ishmael, the solitary whaleman in *Moby Dick*, exclaimed, "There is a fine boisterous something about everything connected with that famous old island." Leave the cars in the driveway, and sit back and relax in a comfortable old chair. Or, if you prefer, put on your walking shoes and tighten up your leg muscles, get on a bike or a horse if you can find one, and prepare yourself for a total Nantucket experience.

1

Historical Context

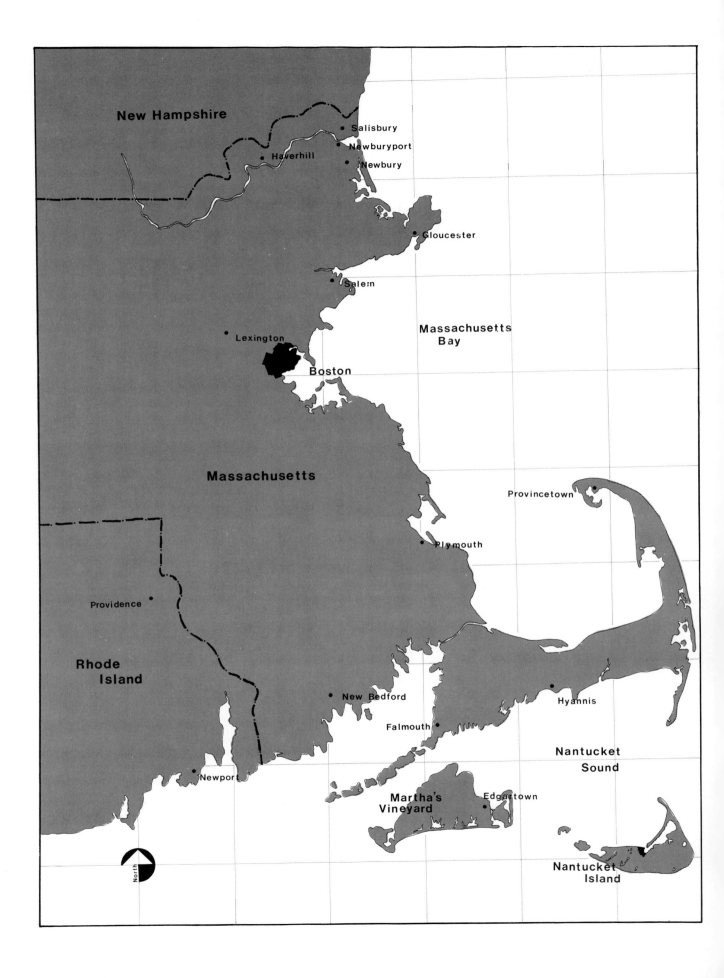

The Land and the Settlers

We shall never really know what it was in 1660 that prompted a small group of English settlers to abandon their homes in the Colonies and sail away to a remote island thirty miles at sea. Surely they were fascinated, as we still are today, with the very idea of an island. The mental images in the minds of those seventeenth-century men and women must have been similar to those we have also pondered, and somewhere in crossing over the Sound, someone, probably a child, must have wondered how Nantucket came to be.

The island Indians had a very simple explanation for the origin of Nantucket. They had a legend about an Indian giant named Maushope, who, many years ago, used Cape Cod for his bed. One night while tossing and turning in his sleep, his moccasins became filled with sand. Filled with rage, he flung them off. One landed close to where he was sleeping and became known as Martha's Vineyard. The other one was tossed further out to sea and became the island of Nantucket.

The Indian word Nantucket means "at the land far out to sea." Most of the names designating portions or communities on the island have evolved from simple Indian words that described the area, or sometimes from the name of the Indian chief who ruled over that section of the island.

Scientists have other explanations for the beginnings of Nantucket. They claim that the island's form, which has been variously described as a hammock, a lamb chop, and an elbow, came about many thousands of years ago during the last glacial age. It was located at the far southern edge and the junction of two major ice fronts. These glaciers helped to form not only Nantucket, but Martha's Vineyard, Cape Cod, and Long Island as well. Earth and stones

were carried by the glaciers and deposited to create the rolling hills that run along the northern part of the island. This morainal area represents the furthest point south of the glacier's movement.

As the ice melted and the glaciers receded, ten thousand years ago, they left a thick layer of debris, called *till*. In some places huge ice blocks remained imbedded, and as these ice blocks melted they left large "kettle holes" throughout the hills. A secondary result of the melting glaciers was the formation of ponds and streams. Icy waters washed the till and sediment down the back slope of the hills to the ocean beyond. The resulting flat and gently sloping areas on the south side of the island are called outwash plains. This area has been heavily scarred by channels from the glacial runoff, and form the valleys to the south shore. Over the course of years, some of these valleys have been blocked by sand, and freshwater or brackish ponds developed behind the natural dams.

Historical Context

The glaciers formed the central body of the island; its final design, however, was created over thousands of years by the winds, rains, and tides. To this very day, these erosional forces shape and reshape the island's perimeter, giving us the scalloped edges of Coatue and the delicate shapes of Great Point, Eel Point, and Smith Point. As a result of the wind and the sea, Nantucket's coastlines are forever changing.

Nantucket Island lies just twenty-two miles south of Cape Cod and is oriented exactly north and south. The use of the terms *right* and *left* seem out of place here; indeed most of the island's residents refer instead to the compass directions of north, south, east and west. It is fourteen miles long and approximately three and a half miles wide, and in this relatively small area we can experience a wide variety of coastlines and landscapes. Nantucket's climate is influenced by the Gulf Stream, which causes the temperatures to average cooler in summer and warmer in winter than on the neighboring mainland.

The earliest sighting of the island was recorded in 1602 by Captain Bartholomew Gosnold, an English seaman. He was bound for Virginia when his course brought him near Cape Cod. A logbook from the voyage contains a simple entry describing "white cliffs" off the coast of the mainland. These white cliffs were Sankaty Head, on the eastern end of Nantucket.

Nearly forty years later, Thomas Mayhew, a missionary from Watertown, Massachusetts, purchased Nantucket and two other smaller islands from the Earl of Stirling. For these he paid forty pounds. Very soon thereafter, Mayhew also secured the deed to Martha's Vineyard and the Elizabeth Islands, and then moved with his family to what is now Edgartown on the Vineyard.

Tristram Coffin, a planter and a land trader from Salisbury, Massachusetts, had heard about the small island near Cape Cod and began to inquire about its availability. With a small group, he visited Mayhew at the Vineyard to begin negotiations. While there, he was introduced to Peter Folger, a surveyor and interpreter to the Indians. Tristram persuaded Folger to join the group, and they pushed on to Nantucket to document the land. The island's purchase from Thomas Mayhew would not guarantee the rights to use the Indian's land; therefore these rights, too, would need to be secured.

At Nantucket there were two great Indian chiefs, or sachems, as they were called: Nickanoose and Wannackmamack. It is believed that when the first Englishmen arrived there were more than a thousand Indians living on the island. They were members of the Narragansett confederation of the Algonquin tribe on the mainland. From the early records we know that they were peaceful, given to farming and fishing rather than fighting. Their numbers seemed to diminish each year. In 1764 a devasting plague all but wiped out the Indian community, reducing their number to fewer than a hundred survivors.

Feeling satisfied at what they found during that first visit, a group of nine settlers, led by Tristram, approached Thomas Mayhew in 1659. Mayhew sold the settlers the patent rights to the island for "the sum of 30 pounds currant pay . . . and also two bever hats, one for my self and one for my wife." He sold all but one tenth of Nantucket to the group, keeping the part known as Quaise for himself.

Tradition tells us that some of these first settlers were seeking to escape religious persecution in the Colonies. During these early years it was against the law in the Massachusetts Bay Colony to be or to entertain the particular religious sect known as Quakers. Many Quakers were branded as heretics and hanged or imprisoned. Non-Quakers who took them in were fined five pounds for every hour a Quaker stayed in their homes. (Considering that the whole of Nantucket Island was sold for thirty pounds, five pounds an hour was a steep fine.) The Puritans of early New England ruled with little tolerance of other religious groups. Although there were no Quakers among the original party of Nantucket settlers—most were either Baptists or Presbyterians—the very idea that a governing group could dictate individual beliefs must have caused some uneasiness in the souls of these independent people. They had, after all, only recently sailed away from an oppressive monarchy in England.

We can guess that freedom must have played a strong role in the founding of Nantucket. It would be a tempting and romantic notion, however, to believe that it was the only reason for leaving the mainland. We know from early records that the purchase of Nantucket was a speculative land deal for Tristram Coffin and the others. Tristram's family owned a lumber mill in New Hampshire, and new houses would certainly mean business for the family. He was a restless man and not new to the world of land trading or settlement. Originally coming to the Colonies from Devonshire, in England, Tristram became one of the first settlers of the town of Newbury, Massachusetts, moving then to settle Haverhill, and finally to Salisbury, County of Essex, in 1642.

Most of the original settlers of Nantucket had emigrated from southeastern England, from Kent, Essex, Southhampton, and Cornwall. Most of them had settled in the County of Essex, and most, like Tristram, were not novices at founding new settlements. Each of the nine men, together with Thomas Mayhew, was allowed to choose a partner to buy in with him. These twenty men became the "First Purchasers" of Nantucket Island:

Thomas Mayhew and partner John Smith
Tristram Coffin and partner Nathanial Starbuck
Thomas Macy and partner Edward Starbuck
Richard Swain and partner Thomas Look
Thomas Barnard and partner Robert Barnard
Peter Coffin and partner James Coffin
Christopher Hussey and partner Robert Pike
Stephen Greenleaf and partner Tristram Coffin, Jr.
John Swain and partner Thomas Coleman
William Pile and partner John Bishop

Look at this list carefully and ponder the question, "How many other communities in America can trace their origins back to the names of the original settlers?" These names have become legendary in Nantucket's history. A brief glance at the island phone book today will reveal the names of people who can trace their roots back to these original twenty men. A simple stone monument in the Historic Cemetery near Maxcy's Pond marks their passing: an entire town has been left to attest their ingenuity.

While Tristram remained in Salisbury, setting up the guidelines for the new settlement, Thomas Macy and his family, Edward Starbuck, and a very young Isaac Coleman spent the winter of 1659–60 on the island. They built their hut at a spot not far from Madaket, close to Eel Point. It was their job to assess the character of the land and decide upon a place to build the first settlement. In addition, they were to continue negotiations with the Indians.

After some exploration, they decided that the settlement might be more ideally suited further to the east, and they chose an area near Capaum Pond (then a harbor) on which to build. In the spring, Edward Starbuck returned to Salisbury with news of the island. Eight to ten families returned with him to Nantucket, traveling between May 10 and July 15, 1660. Not all of the first purchasers chose to relocate to the island. Tristram Coffin, Jr., and William Pile, for instance, never came to Nantucket.

We can only imagine what it must have been like to step off those boats more than three hundred years ago. The children must have thought it a grand adventure; the adults, on the other hand, must have doubted their original intentions more than once. The remote windswept setting did not offer a hospitable environment for crops or pasture. The salt air and the strong occasional nor'easters, with winds sometimes reaching sixty to ninety miles per hour, have overcome even well-established trees. Only the most determined plant life has survived for our enjoyment. Because of the sparse vegetation, we can speculate that those early settlers were even more aware than we are today of being on an island, completely surrounded by water. There were not many beautiful trees or foliage as there are now to block the views of the ocean.

We can ascertain from many sources—Melville, Emerson, de Crevecoeur, and others—that two centuries after the first settlers, in the mid-nineteenth century, there was still little or no cultivated vegetation on Nantucket. Thoreau wrote in 1854 that "There is not a tree to be seen except such as are set out about houses . . . This island must look exactly like a prairie, except that the view in clear weather is bounded by the sea. . . ." [1]

The very early records, however, list many references to trees or woods. The tract of land near the Head of Hummock Pond was traditionally called "the Long Woods." In the town records of 1676 it is written that "no more green wood shall be felled in the Long Woods except what is taken for rails and fence." The Indian word *Coatue* means "land of the pine woods." Excavations, too, have yielded evidence of there being large oaks on the island at one time. Early historians believed that there might have been trees large enough to furnish wood for the houses of the first settlers, but by the turn of the eighteenth century, lumber was being brought over from the mainland, most notably from New Hampshire and Maine.

Out of the first settlers, Tristram emerged as a very strong and vocal leader. He was naturally more knowledgeable than most about land trading, and he was able to control five of the original twenty shares. (In addition to his own share, his three sons and his son-in-law, Stephen Greenleaf, were among the First Purchasers.) He was appointed first Chief Magistrate of Nantucket, presiding over local affairs and representing the island in royal government business.

Very early on, it became evident that if they were to build a community, the Nantucketers would need the help of certain tradesmen. As most of the settlers were farmers, they needed to import a skilled labor force. The First Purchasers offered half-shares in the island to skilled craftsmen such as fishermen, carpenters, coopers, cobblers, and tailors. The new settlers who responded came from as far away as England and as close as Martha's Vineyard. The Gardners, the Worths, the Mitchells and others came to work their crafts on Nantucket. There were fourteen of these "Half-Share" men in all. Two stand out perhaps more than the rest.

Captain John Gardner, whose lone tombstone stands in the Historic Cemetery, was an outspoken leader for the half-share men, often coming to blows with Tristram Coffin. In fact, he succeeded Tristram as Chief Magistrate of Nantucket.

Peter Folger, introduced before, was convinced to move from

---

the Vineyard and act as an interpreter to the Nantucket Indians. He played a strong role in the forming and settling of the island, as did his children. Peter's youngest daughter, named Abiah, was born at Nantucket, and would become the mother of Benjamin Franklin.

This system of First Purchasers and Half-Share men, although rational enough in concept, never worked entirely well in reality. During the first thirty years, several revolts and bitter power struggles broke out between the First Purchasers, led by Tristram, and the Half-Share men, led by John Gardner. These arguments dominated much of Nantucket's early settlement until around the turn of the eighteenth century. It was left to succeeding generations to smooth the difficulties created by their fathers.

The records speak of the two families being reconciled by the marriage of John Gardner's daughter, Mary, to Tristram's grandson, Jethro. The young couple's house still stands in its original location on Sunset Hill. Known today as Nantucket's Oldest House, it was built in 1686 as a wedding gift from the couple's fathers. The Gardners supplied the land, and the Coffins the lumber. Tradition tells us that the wedding was held up because Jethro's father wanted to see the deed to the property and Mary's father had neglected to transfer it to his soon-to-be son-in-law. There was no wedding until the documents were signed. As soon as the paperwork was completed to the Coffins' satisfaction, Jethro and Mary were married with their fathers' skeptical, but bountiful blessings. Perhaps this house should be seen as a symbol of peace that united two very strong and independent families.

What kind of men and women settled this desolate island more than three hundred years ago? The early Nantucketers were simple people, individualists, with a common interest in the community. Most were not followers, but instead leaders, explorers, and chance-takers. Like the many immigrants who have fled to America over the years, those earliest pioneers saw an opportunity for a better way of life for themselves and their families. Their colorful legends have outlived them by three centuries. Interwoven with the names and deeds of the settlers of Nantucket are countless other names and deeds of people who have never set foot on the island, but have touched its meaning in some mystical way. It is a universal theme. This was the spirit that founded America.

Evolution of the Town

■Like many other towns in the Commonwealth of Massachusetts, Nantucket began with a Proprietary. The twenty First Purchasers, together with the fourteen Half-Share men formed a Proprietary of twenty-seven original shareholders. Nearly all of the first inhabitants of Nantucket were partners in this large corporation, which was based upon a common interest in the betterment of the community as a whole. Land was more or less divided equally, distributed in some areas, and held in common in others. Although they had formed a Proprietary when the patent rights had been transferred from Thomas Mayhew, it was not until after the turn of the eighteenth century that they were called "The Proprietors of the Common and Undivided Lands of Nantucket." Prior to that, they referred to themselves as "freeholders."

Sheep farming was to be the occupation of the Nantucket freeholders, and the division of land was based on the number of sheep that it could support. Certain tracts were set off for individual uses, while the bulk of the island was kept in common and given over to the sheep. The Proprietors had a rather simple method of apportioning land originally; however, the method became ever more complicated over time. Many explanations survive of how the land at Nantucket was divided. In many cases the explanations have grown as complicated as the system itself. The following explanation, though lengthy, is perhaps one of the simplest.

The smallest unit of land in the Proprietary was called a sheep's common. In the beginning, the settlers reasoned that it took about an acre and a half to pasture one sheep, and that was the measure of one sheep's common. The total available land amounted to about 29,000 acres, so if all of the land on Nantucket were held in common, a total of 19,440 sheep could be pastured comfortably. This amounted to 720 sheep's commons for each of the twenty-seven proprietors, or $^{720}/_{19,440}$ of the common land.

The first purchasers bought the principal Indian rights in two deeds from the two sachems, then, over a period of time, purchased deeds from individual Indian owners. The last deed was dated 1774. As quickly as land was purchased from the Indians, large tracts were laid out to form "divisions." The Proprietors laid out many of these divisions and designated them by such names as Squam, Wesko, Smooth Hummocks, and others. Each of these, unlike the common land, was subdivided into twenty-seven shares as nearly equal in size as possible, *quality and quantity considered.* Lots were cast to determine which share of the new division each proprietor would receive. This was called "dividend land."

The proprietors laid out these parcels in severalty in order that each shareholder could use his plot as he wanted. The amount of land in these shares varied depending on the full size of the division, though each proprietor always received one twenty-seventh of the total. Parcels could be as small as the Warehouse division shares of two and a half square rods (a rod being sixteen and a half feet), or as great as the Southeast Quarter shares of ninety-one acres.

Each proprietor always had an equal one-twenty-seventh of the dividend land and $^{720}/_{19,440}$ of the common land. Shares in dividend land could be bought and sold, used as doweries or bartered, but the common land was not negotiable for trade. We can only imagine what happened when the children of the original proprietors acquired these shares by inheritance or marriage. For instance, one son of ten children of one of the original proprietors might find himself with one-tenth of his father's holdings, or seventy-two sheep's commons ($^{72}/_{19,440}$ of the common land); a grandson might have only $^{8}/_{19,440}$, and a great-grandson, $^{4}/_{19,440}$. This is when the complications set in, for these "sheep's commons" never actually indicated anything definite in area or value, rather they represented a certain undivided fractional interest in an unspecified area of the island. Moreover, as the dividend land was established, the total common land bank dropped. Furthermore, if a portion of the dividend land was to be sold, it became nearly impossible to locate all of the shareholders and their heirs having claim to that portion.

In 1815, the Massachusetts Supreme Court ended all interest in common by authorizing ownership transferred to individuals in exchange for sheep's commons rights. If an individual owned at least 100 sheep's commons (or 150 acres), he could require the Proprietary to set off his land in one place. His interest in the common land, then, would be exchanged for this specific piece of property. Gradually all

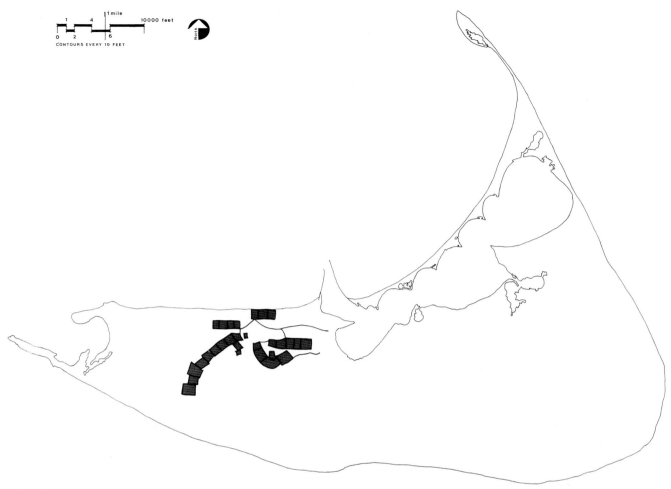

Sherborne, 1665

of the common land on Nantucket Island was set off and purchased
in this way.

On the mainland, back in 1659, the first order of business in the
Proprietary was to lay out the house-share lots. These were apportioned by Tristram, Peter Folger, and others. Each Proprietor then
cast lots to see which plot he would receive. Most of the lots contained on the average sixty square rods, or about twenty acres each.
Half-share men received a plot of land roughly half the size of a full
shareholder's land.

The house lots were clustered in one location so that the remaining portion of the island could stay in common ownership and be
used for agriculture and grazing sheep. The Proprietors chose a
settlement site about one and a half miles west of what is now Nantucket Town, centered among Capaum Pond, Washing Pond, and
Maxcy's Pond. The house lots radiated out, extending as far south as

the fork in Hummock Pond. The central focus was the meeting house, the home of Mary and Nathanial Starbuck, called Parliament House.

At this time, the island fell under the jurisdiction of the Royal Province of New York, to which Nantucket paid "four barrels mercantible codfish" annually. Francis Lovelace, the Royal Governor, named the new village Sherborne in 1673. Today, only the Elihu Coleman house remains in its original setting on the old Coleman homestead near the head of Hummock Pond. In times gone by, we could explore the perimeter of the ponds for signs of these early homes. There used to be a marker at the head of Capaum Pond where Tristram's house might have stood, but now even that is gone, fallen victim to the playing winds and sands.

After the first house lots were laid out, grazing and meadow lands were apportioned. As the Proprietary's interest was already turning toward the sea, an area near the Great Harbor was the next to be divided in 1678. This area was called Wesko, or Wescoe, which means "bright, or white, stone" in the Indian dialect. It comprised twenty acres in the center of today's town. The original division was bounded by Federal, Liberty, North Liberty and Broad streets. Land was divided east and west into twenty narrow strips, eighty rods long and two rods wide, with each strip having an end on the harbor. Federal Street at that time marked the water's edge. Historians have often remarked that the appearance of these divisions resembled yardsticks. The other seven shareholders were given land elsewhere to make a total of twenty-seven shares.

The village of Sherborne flourished until just after the turn of the eighteenth century, when a sandbar formed across the entrance to Capaum Harbor. By 1720, the harbor was completely closed. After numerous discussions, residents decided to move the town east to the Great Harbor. Many of the original houses at Capaum Pond were dismantled, put on carts, and rebuilt in Wescoe. Some were moved whole; of others only pieces, such as doors, windows, or parts of the structure were used.

Prior to the move to the Great Harbor, three events happened that would influence the island community's future development. First, in 1693, William and Mary transferred Nantucket and Martha's Vineyard from the Royal Government of New York to the Massachusetts Bay Colony. Unlike in New York, Massachusetts law provided each man in the community with an equal vote and say in local politics. This decision severely weakened the power of the Proprietary, which until that time exerted the sole control over island affairs.

The second event took place a few years into the new century, when traveling Quaker missionaries visited Nantucket on their way to the mainland. Restrictions against Quakers had lessened some-

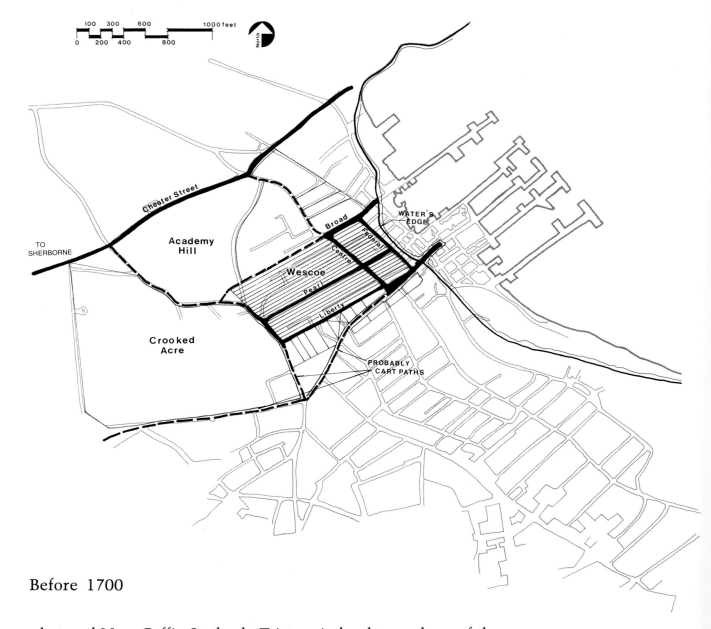

Before 1700

what, and Mary Coffin Starbuck, Tristram's daughter and one of the most influential people in town, was sympathetic to their growing movement. She converted to the faith and became one of the foremost preachers on the island. Her home hosted many Quaker First Day meetings.

It is thought that the name *Quaker* was first applied to the Society of Friends in 1650, when George Fox, then the leader of the movement, was brought before the magistrates of Derby, England. Mr. Fox admonished the magistrates for their worldliness, and said that instead they should "quake at the name of the Lord." One of the magistrates, Gervose Bennett, remembered this outburst, and Fox himself later said that Mr. Bennett "was the first to call us Quakers." The Society of Friends, as they called themselves, spread rapidly on Nantucket, reaching its peak growth around the turn of the nineteenth century, when half of the population was of that belief. Their numbers included the wealthiest and most influential families on the island.

The Friends believed in an "inner light," and that this inner spirit "lighteneth every man that cometh into the world." They spoke with the soft *thees* and *thous* of old English, abhorred violence of any nature, and believed in the basic equality of everyone. Today, we can scarcely believe the tyranny with which the followers of this gentle philosophy ruled Nantucket and dominated all public life for more than a hundred years.

The Quaker intolerance of "the World's People" and material possessions pervaded their society. Beauty for beauty's sake was seen as evil. In their dress, their buildings, and in all outward appearances, they remained simple and humble. Utility and function triumphed over art and beauty. Long after the rest of the world had abandoned building styles and fashions, the Quakers tenaciously clung to them, with an intolerance to the end for earthly comforts of any kind. It was this very intolerance that led to their downfall. The great schism in the Society of Friends occurred around 1830. Gradually, in their dress, their architecture, and spirit—willing or not—they joined the World's People. As had been often reminded at Quaker meeting, "pride goeth before a fall."

On upper Main Street, in the Old Quaker Cemetery lie between nine and ten thousand Quakers, buried with no markers and no memory to their names. Such was their intolerance for earthly symbols that it accompanied them even to the grave.

The third event leading to Nantucket's great changes during the eighteenth century was the sighting of a whale in Nantucket Harbor. The whale was harpooned, and, albeit modestly, the whale-catching industry had begun. The settlers, accompanied by the Indians, soon began hunting the whale offshore in small open boats. By the middle of the eighteenth century, most of the citizens on the island were engaged in some way in the pursuit of whales. To support this new industry, small businesses sprang up: ropewalks (long covered buildings where ropes were manufactured), iron foundries, cooper's shops, warehouses, and ship's carpenters. Although it began slowly, whaling evolved into the most prosperous industry on Nantucket.

With both whaling and the Quaker movement in their infancies, the town was relocated to the Great Harbor. This village, too, was

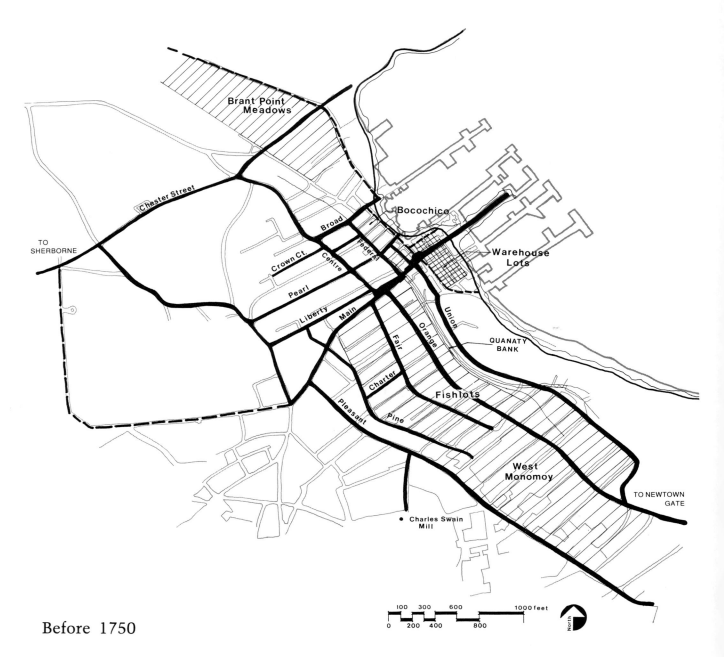

Before 1750

known as Sherborne until 1795, when it was officially changed
to Nantucket. The exact locations of the dividend lands in town are
difficult to ascertain today. The eighteenth-century custom of marking and recording land according to natural landmarks, such as rocks
or trees, and corners or walls of neighboring houses (which may or
may not be here now) has proven confusing, and frustrating to
twentieth-century researchers. In addition, many of the individuals
chosen to lay out the new tracts were not surveyors by trade.

The new town by the harbor grew rapidly, as everyone wanted

to be near the water. After the Wescoe Acres Subdivision, the Fish-lots were the next tract laid out in 1717. These were south of Main Street, and continued south to today's Eagle Lane. The twenty-seven lots were all oriented toward Fair Street, which was laid out down the middle of the tract. They extended west to Pine Street and east to the Quanaty Bank, later to Orange Street. Unlike the narrow Wescoe Lots, these averaged 116 feet wide.

Following the Fishlots, the West Monomoy division was opened in 1726, directly south of the Fishlots. Orange Street was extended south from Main to act as the eastern boundary, and Pleasant Street was created for the western boundary. These twenty-seven lots were somewhat narrower than the Fishlots.

The town was beginning to take shape. Main Street was an important hinge linking the north and south divisions, and as the principal highway to the harbor. The original Straight Wharf was laid out a few years into the eighteenth century, and was, in effect, a continuation of Main Street out into the harbor. As the whaling industry progressed, the Proprietors recognized the value of land adjacent to the water. Small Warehouse Divisions were laid out in 1723. These were valuable shares that ran between Pearl Street and Main Street, and measured only sixteen by forty feet apiece.

The other locations near the water were quickly subdivided. The area bounded by Main Street, Federal Street, and today's South Water Street was at one time under water. The proprietors worked to reclaim the land. Then they leveled and laid out the new street after the water receded. It was called the Bocochico[2] and was subdivided for commercial ventures in 1746. The Water Lots were laid out north and south in two divisions: first in 1765, then in 1805.

The town expanded in direct proportion to the growth of the whaling industry. It ceased to be a rural village composed primarily of farmers and sheep owners and instead evolved into a prosperous cosmopolitan center, communicating and trading with the world. This was no small unknown island in the Atlantic, for it was Nantucket whale oil that lit the streets of Europe, and her whalemen were welcomed the world over.

Eventually the immediate waters were all but depleted of whales, and Nantucketers were forced to go further and further to sea to find the large herds. Although briefly set back by the Revolutionary War, the Nantucket whalers pressed on. First they discovered the rich territories off the coast of Brazil. Then, in 1791, the ship *Beaver* rounded Cape Horn and opened a gateway to the Pacific for Nantucket ships. This was followed by the opening of the whaling grounds off the coast of Japan in the second quarter of the nineteenth century.

Before 1800

Whaling voyages by this time lasted upwards of three years. Larger ships were necessary for the longer voyages, perpetuating the need for more shops on the island; thus, the Nantucket whaling industry exploded by the turn of the nineteenth century. For that brief moment in history, there were more millionaires living on the tiny island than anywhere else in the world. The Quakers and their humble

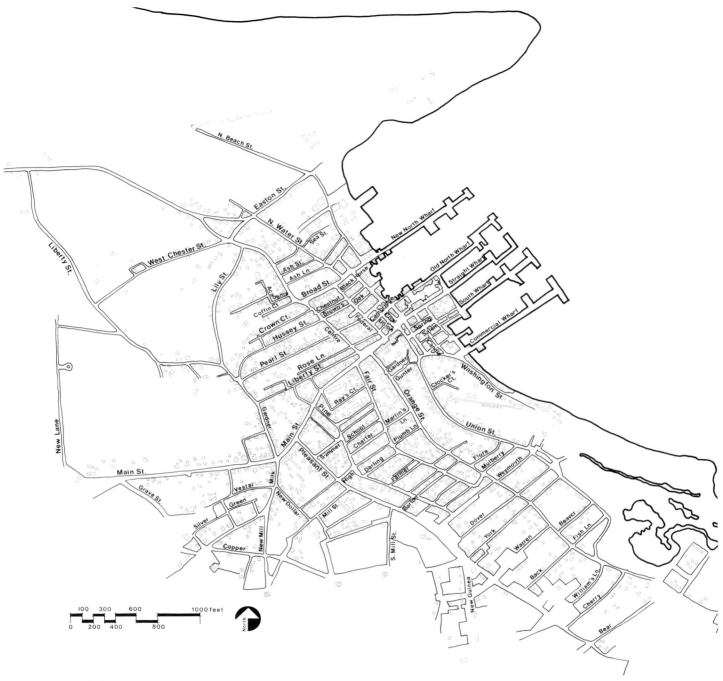

In 1834

existence were fast dying out, replaced by a life style that not only
included, but supported, the World's People.

Just as prosperity was reaching its peak, however, Nantucket
suffered her worst setback since the War of 1812. On July 13, 1846,

Area Destroyed by the Great Fire, 1846

a fire broke out on Main Street, beginning in the hat store belonging to William Geary. The devastation raged all night, and by the following morning, one million dollars' worth of damage had been done and one-third of the town center destroyed. All of the wharves except Commercial Wharf lay in ashes. When dawn broke, the harbor waters were still ablaze with oil, and merchants could only stand back and watch with horror as their precious cargoes turned to smoke and ashes.[3]

In the town, the fire was contained by four brick structures: the Pacific Bank and the Folger block on the west end of Main Street Square, the brick dwelling at number 5 Orange Street, and the Jared Coffin house on Broad Street to the north. Had it not been for these brick buildings, we can only guess how many other buildings might have succumbed to the fire.

The Nantucketers wasted no time in rebuilding their town. The north side of Main Street was pushed further north to straighten and widen the principal street to ninety feet. Federal and Centre Streets were also widened; however, many of the smaller lanes, such as Brown's Lane and Blackhorse Lane, were never recreated. Following the Great Fire, trees were imported to line the new streets. The elms on Main Street were planted in 1851 by Charles and Henry Coffin, direct descendants of old Tristram. The English maples were planted on Centre Street by N.A. Sprague.

The late nineteenth century brought many smaller plants, hedges, bushes, and flowers into the town's gardens and streets. Much of the lush foliage seen today was first planted after the Great Fire of 1846. Also around this time, trees from the Orient were introduced by Pacific whaling men and China trading vessels. Pagoda, ginko, and Chinese elm trees can be seen sporadically throughout the town.

The contemporary street pattern in the old town was developed from the original lot layouts for the dividend land. Streets evolved from property lines, working or radiating out from the center (or Wescoe Acres). On the whole, the entire town as we see it today was completely intact by the mid-nineteenth century.

Just after the town had recovered from the Great Fire, the island would be dealt her greatest difficulties. Kerosene was developed and oil found in the hills of Pennyslvania. Almost overnight, the whaling industry became obsolete. A vast depression encircled Nantucket like a dense permanent fog, throwing thousands of residents out of work. Many took down their houses, loaded them on ships, and left for the Gold Rush in California, others settled permanently on the New England mainland. The final blow was dealt her by the American Civil War. Some of the Nantucketers remained

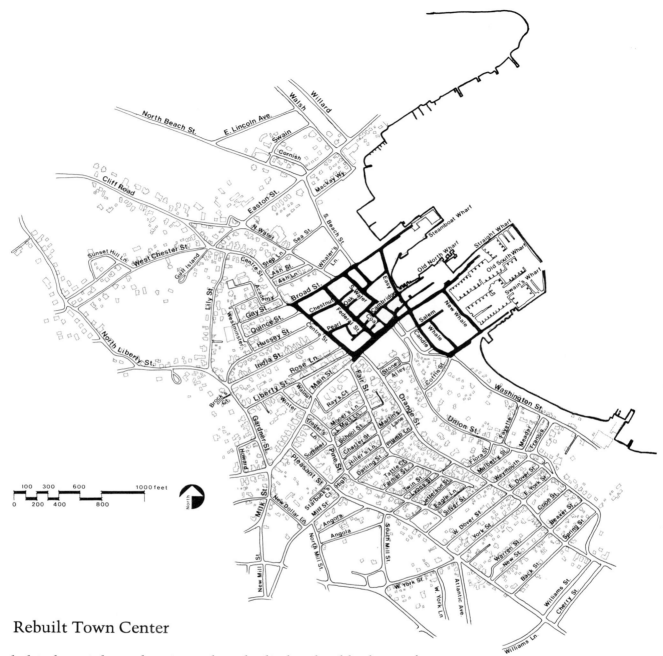

Rebuilt Town Center

behind to pick up the pieces, but the little island had gone fast to sleep. And like Rip van Winkle, she stayed asleep for almost fifty years, completely missing the Industrial Revolution and the advent of factory production, until the American leisure class discovered her as a summer playground.

Whaling was replaced by the new tourist industry in the late 1800s, when steamboat service commenced, thus linking the islands with Woods Hole on the mainland. In 1881 the Nantucket Railroad extended from Commercial Wharf along Washington Street to Surf-side, then out to 'Sconset, transporting the summer visitors all over the island. By the end of the nineteenth century, Nantucket had come fully alive in an age of great hotels and summer elegance. Many of the people who came to the island for the summer months returned every year with their children, and their children's children. Some bought the old deserted houses in town, made friends with the ghosts, and renovated the little gray structures; still others built their new summer mansions out on the Cliff and on the bluffs at 'Sconset.

This was a gracious time of white suits, straw hats, and para-sols. For a brief moment, there was peace throughout most of the world. Albeit fleeting, it was almost magic. It should come as no surprise that the leisure class of New England chose Nantucket, which whaling money had built and Quaker tenacity had preserved, as their playground. It should also come as no surprise that these people chose to stay on long after the summer months had ended.

Evolution of the Architecture

As we walk down the streets and lanes of old Nantucket, we can see in the buildings a form of three-dimensional history, a collage of time, where layers of generations have been built side by side. We can call forth the time in which a certain building flourished just by recognizing a few key elements of its composition, or its style; however, the meaning of architecture is really more than the identification of styles by visual cues. We can imagine that each house was in tune to the specific concept and rhythm of a specific era. Styles develop, like cultures, over long periods of time, never completely emerging all at once.

The interior spatial patterns, exterior architectural forms, and building methods evolved more slowly on Nantucket than on the mainland. The simple forms of the earliest houses influenced the activities of the first inhabitants and those of the succeeding generation, which in turn modified or added to the house and influenced the following one, and so forth.

Additions can be seen on nearly every house in the old town. On Nantucket, these additions are affectionately called "warts." We are allowed to visualize in each house the family's growth and prosperity, as additions to the family promoted additions to the house. The original settlers began with one-room cottages. Soon it became necessary to add other rooms. At first, borning rooms, chambers, and more children's sleeping rooms were added; later came a separate kitchen, called a porch.

Because the majority of Nantucket's houses were set directly on the street's edge, the only place to enlarge was to the rear, or sometimes to the side. This restriction helped to create today's beautiful streets and lanes, which are lined by many original building

facades. These stern "public" faces seem very formal when compared with the houses' "private" faces to the rear, filled with
additions, porches, decks, and clotheslines. In short, the backs of
these houses represent complete asymmetrical pictures of family life.

The creation of architecture is almost always influenced by
external sources. In addition to practical needs and site constraints,
there are politics, economics, social values, and materials at hand to
affect the building of any structure. Nantucket's architecture was
largely shaped by its remote site and the prevailing culture. The most
obvious influence came from the sea and shipbuilding. Up until the
nineteenth century, the majority of buildings were built by ship's
carpenters, and it was not unusual for a peculiar nautical device to
find its way into house construction. For example, many houses have
doors with top edges that slant; some have beams supported by
"ship's knees," a particular wooden angle brace formed by the trunk
and root of a tree and used, as the name implies, in the construction
of ships. Houses were "clinker built": just as the external planks of
a ship overlap each other and help push down the waves, the
shingles or clapboards of the houses are good protection against the

Nantucket "warts"
near Fair Street.

Evolution of the Architecture

25

strong winter winds and rains. The often severe climate also required that the structures be compact in order to retain heat. Externally as well as internally, the little houses exhibit the balance, proportion, and efficiency of seaworthy vessels. Perhaps they can best be understood as land-based ships in a peaceful ocean of sand.

A strong sense of provincialism and insularity slowed the progression of architecture on Nantucket. This reluctance to adopt the ways of the World's People began with the Quakers, but to some degree, all island cultures have a solidarity about them. On Nantucket, even to this very day, the mainland is sometimes referred to simply as "the continent," or in some cases, "over in America." The island's very remoteness was its insulation against the world. News and information, even when it came, was often late.

The same ocean that caused Nantucket's isolation would later provide her main source of income. The Quaker whaling men saw houses as a secondary extravagance; their extra money went into the fitting and refitting of ships. In their zealousness, they clung to styles and manners of building that were long out of date on the mainland. Moreover, because of the costliness of transporting materials across Nantucket Sound, many of the earliest houses were taken down, put on carts, and reassembled when the original town was relocated to the Great Harbor just before 1720. Doors, windows, and building structures were used over and over again, making the precise dating and style of many houses difficult, if not impossible.

The Quakers and the sea left an indelible mark on Nantucket architecture, but we shall see that each succeeding generation had its say in turn. Through architecture, we can trace the entire civilization of the island. Of course, the true experience of architecture lies within its spaces. Today we are allowed to participate only by imagining what it might have been like to dwell within these rooms. And because it is difficult for us to actually visit these interiors, we will concentrate primarily on the building's exterior presence and the space it inhabits on the street and in the community.[4]

Architectural History as Experienced on Main Street

A casual stroll down Main Street will reveal nearly the entire history of architecture on Nantucket.

 The Beginning

The Medieval Cottage, 1600–1700 (139 Main Street).
The original sources for the first American houses were the small cottages that dotted the English countryside in the early 1600s. The earliest houses of the first white settlers on Nantucket were patterned after those simple Medieval structures that the Colonists had left behind. As vegetation was rare on the island, the cottages were often huddled together to act as windbreaks, and as natural building materials were scarce, the houses remained small and snug. The floor plans, at first, were only one room deep, and a great fireplace was placed in the center to provide heat.

To take full advantage of the sun's daily path, these houses traditionally faced south. Most also had small side gardens, like their English predecessors. The structural system was wooden post-and-beam, introduced to the Colonies by master craftsmen. A form of exterior weatherboarding was common in the Southeastern part of England, and this method, too, made its way across the Atlantic. These were massive vertical or horizontal boards, not overlapped as clapboards are, but butted against one another. This device was initially used for roofs as well as walls. The interiors were also sealed and insulated using a crude form of wattle-and-daub made up of clamshell paste.

The first houses had steeply pitched roofs, originally designed for the use of thatch and the English climate. The extreme pitch was

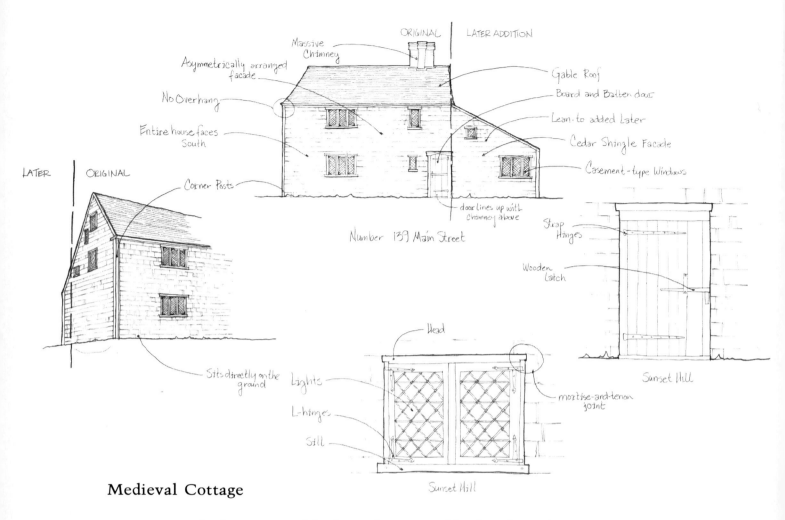

Medieval Cottage

necessary to shed water quickly from the permeable thatch. Early on in America, wooden shakes replaced thatch, and even though water did not soak through the shingles as quickly as it did thatch, the roof pitch stayed the same. There were no overhangs on these roofs, because the strong northeast winds would have caught the underside and sheared the roof edge off. In addition, there was a practical solar concern for the absence of overhangs. Due to Nantucket's mild summers, the settlers had little need for summer shading, but in winter they welcomed the sun's low rays.

Glass was an extravagance in the seventeenth century and often hard to come by. Light was provided through small leaded casement windows, placed wherever they were needed the most, as view and aesthetics were not really a consideration in the beginning. A tall, massive chimney, usually built of handmade brick, towered above the small rooftop.

A good example of this Medieval English cottage can be found at 139 Main Street. It originally stood on Crooked Acre, the land

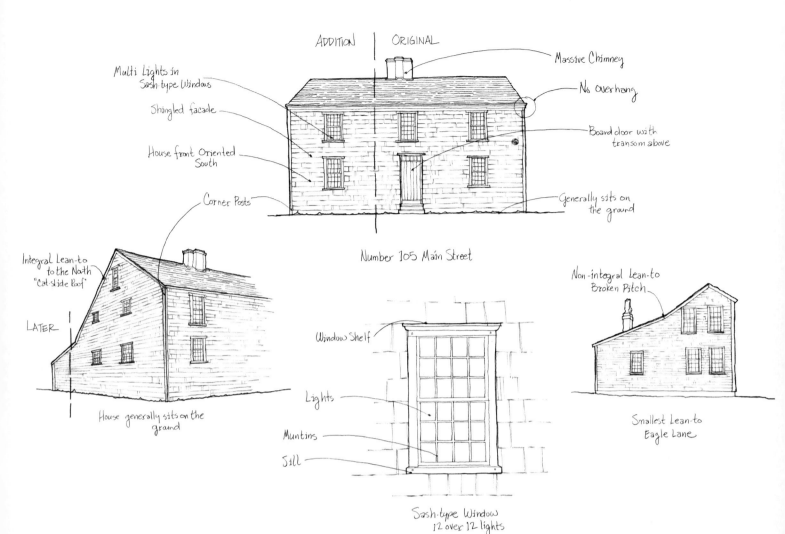

ADDITION | ORIGINAL

Multi Lights in Sash-type Windows

Shingled facade

House front Oriented South

Corner Posts

Massive Chimney

No overhang

Board door with transom above

Generally sits on the ground

Number 105 Main Street

Integral Lean-to to the North "Cat-slide Roof"

LATER

House generally sits on the ground

Window Shelf

Lights

Muntins

Sill

Sash-type Window
12 over 12 lights

Non-integral Lean-to
Broken Pitch

Smallest Lean-to
Eagle Lane

The Lean-to

deeded to Richard Gardner in the early Proprietary. This tiny cottage was built prior to 1700 for either Richard Gardner or his son. The original plan was a single great room with a sleeping chamber above. The shed addition on the east side as well as the lean-to on the rear were added later in the eighteenth century. Until 1928, the time of its restoration, the building stood about five hundred feet from its present site and functioned as a carriage house for another residence.

The Lean-to, 1680–1750 (105 Main Street). The house at 139 Main Street looks very much like a Lean-to, the next evolution of the Nantucket house. This modest structure was called a "saltbox" on the mainland, because in the early eighteenth century its shape resembled a particular type of salt container. Its tall front and lower rear wall produced what has sometimes been called a "catslide" roof.

As has been mentioned, the earliest cottages were modified by the addition of a "wart." This usually consisted of a lean-to addition to the rear, or in some cases to the side, of the house. To the great rooms were added a chamber, a borning room, and sometimes a smaller milk room. This addition quickly became integral with the original construction. In looking at the expanse of roof to the rear of a Lean-to house, we can speculate which of these warts were actual later additions and which were planned with the original construction. Those which were added make a slight break in the long rear roof pitch, whereas the ones that were part of the original construction present a continuous roof slope on the north side.

The street system in Nantucket developed over a long period, and most of these early Lean-tos were not compelled to line up with a street, as the houses of the next generation would be. Instead, it was customary to orient them by ship's compass, with the entrance and principal rooms to the south. The catslide roof faced north to deflect the cold winds. Often the kitchen or buttery was in the cooler rear part of the building. Our forefathers were quick to learn basic solar concepts and apply them to building design.

The Lean-tos were generally of two sizes. A small one, close in proportion to the English cottage, had the chimney aligned with the front door. The larger was, in effect, a double version of the smaller house. When the smaller Lean-to was doubled, it was as if the fireplace acted as a pivot, with the newer portion, a mirror image of the original, revolving around to the other side of it. The fireplace could then easily heat both halves. These are massive fireplaces, in some cases they are more than nine feet wide and tall enough to walk into.

Window panes—or lights, as they are called—remained small, though the window form had evolved into a larger, double-hung sash type, and the overall composition of windows was becoming ordered on the facade.

After the turn of the eighteenth century, better tools allowed the Colonists to cut wooden shakes, and these thin shingles replaced the earlier form of weatherboarding. They were used for roofs as well as walls.

Religion was the central point around which Nantucket society revolved. All of life was caught up in the Quaker's First Day meetings. The Lean-to house suited the Quaker purpose nicely, as it had the Puritans on the mainland. It was simple, economical, and exhibited to the outside world a humbleness that paralleled the somber Quaker dress. They believed that a house, like clothing, should be mainly concerned with utility; beauty was only an accidental by-product of the functionalism. Lavish displays of architecture, like buttons and bows, were only for the World's People. According to Obed Macy, an early historian, the Quakers only used paint when it was necessary for the protection and preservation of the wood. During the eighteenth century, most of the houses and their trim were painted a rust red. White paint was not readily available until much later, for it was costly to refine white lead. Despite the expense, most houses on the mainland sported white trim. The Quakers, however, in their zeal to avoid extravagance, continued to use red paint for many years.

The house facing the Civil War monument at 105 Main Street is a very good example of an early Lean-to modified into a double house. The eastern portion was built about 1690 at Capaum Harbor. When the harbor closed, the house was taken down and moved to its present location. It was easier to dismantle houses then because buildings were constructed not with nails, but with wooden pegs and mortise-and-tenon joints. The western portion was added on for Christopher Starbuck and his family after the house had been moved. Its two-story front is oriented due south, as Main Street was not yet the bustling avenue that it would later become.

The Typical Nantucket House, 1750–1820 (127 Main Street). Often the Lean-to continued to be modified until the additions covered more area than the original structure. Families were large and prolific. In the eighteenth century Quaker families began to recognize that they needed more space. The next evolution of the Nantucket house was a dramatic spatial modification: the rear wall was heightened to two full stories, eliminating the catslide roof.

Not all of the Friends were pleased with this new development. Many stories have been handed down of certain Quakers attempting to suppress this change. Two accounts seem to be the most popular. In 1790, Job Macy was building his house on Mill Street, at the corner of New Dollar Lane. When his father discovered that Job intended to build his house with two stories in the front and back, thereby eliminating the characteristic lean-to roof, he swore that if his son built in this newfangled style he (the father) would never step foot in the house. Tradition holds that he never did. We have to admire the perseverance of this eighteenth-century Job. Another Quaker was not so courageous when it was discovered that his house near Stone Alley was being built with a frame brought over from the mainland—one with a full two stories, front and rear. In no time, the overseers were dispatched, and the owner was convinced, through threat of disassociation, to cut down the back portion of the second story.

This new change threatened to disrupt the entire community. Its ostentatiousness was widely debated at meeting; nevertheless, even the most stubborn had to admit that the new structural system would allow a greater spaciousness *and usefulness* in the interior. It was the new style's very functionalism that saved it.

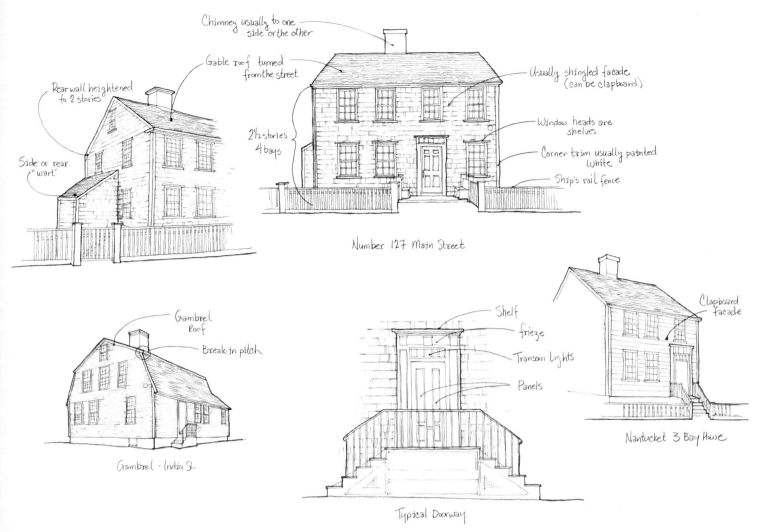

Chimney usually to one side or the other

Gable roof turned from the street

Rear wall heightened to 2 stories

Side or rear "wart"

2½ stories 4 bays

Usually shingled facade (can be clapboard)

Window heads are shelves

Corner trim usually painted white

Ship's rail fence

Number 127 Main Street

Gambrel Roof

Break in pitch

Gambrel - India St.

Shelf

frieze

Transom Lights

Panels

Typical Doorway

Clapboard facade

Nantucket 3 Bay House

Typical Nantucket House

The once small village was fast becoming a bustling town by the late eighteenth century. The sand cart-paths and dividend lot separations were being recognized as public streets, and as a result, it became important to align the house fronts with them. Housewrights abandoned the earlier custom of always facing the house south. In town, the houses were placed close to one another and set directly on the street's edge. Albeit a minor change, the new custom of aligning houses with the street rather than by the sun was the first outward gesture in the rather introverted building style of Nantucket Quakers. True to their rigid code of behavior, nearly everyone complied with the new arrangement once it got started, and the abundance of these streetside houses indicates the growth of the Society of Friends in the eighteenth century.

The house at 127 Main Street is a later example of the Nantucket Typical house. It is characteristic of Nantucket houses that flourished between 1750 and 1820. The front and rear wall are two full stories. The total form comprises two and a half stories and is four window bays wide. Some houses were raised up on modest stone foundations, and most were consistently built eighteen to twenty feet tall. The gabled roof was still without any overhang or dormers; however, roof walks were beginning to appear. The faces of these houses were asymmetrically balanced, with the door and chimney typically located to one side or the other. Unique projecting window and door shelves were used, giving a shadow distinction to the upper line of these openings. This was the only outward form of ornamentation. The entire house was covered with cedar shingles, left to weather gray, and outlined with red or white trim.

The interior contains a feature peculiar to Nantucket: transoms, like those found over front doors, were also used over interior doors. This device was thought by many to help in quickly spotting interior fires, a necessity in a town where the majority of structures were built entirely of wood.

Some Typical Nantucket houses have gambrel roofs. This was a Dutch construction from the late Middle Ages transported across the Atlantic. The gambrel roof, rather than being a continuous roof pitch like the gable, breaks to become even steeper. Basically the floor plan of a Gambrel was very similar to that of a Typical Nantucket house, but the top floor was much more spacious. In addition, because of its unique construction, a Gambrel house did not require as much building material; thus, owners could economize. Moreover, in the early Colonies, property taxes were levied according to the number of stories, and a gambrel roof would allow the best of both opportunities. It appeared to be a single story, but was in fact a very usable two-story building.

The idea had to have been popular with the conservative Quakers, yet very few original Gambrels survive today. Old paintings, done prior to the Great Fire of 1846, show several Gambrels in the town center. Most were commercial buildings. The Pacific Club, for instance, at the foot of Main Street, was originally a Gambrel structure, but its roof line was changed and heightened after the fire.

Many slight variations of these Typical Nantucket houses can be seen about town. Sometimes the house had only three window bays. Often the window sizes or locations were subtly varied, and sometimes one or two windows were omitted altogether. Mostly, however, these simple structures conformed in size and shape to a predetermined role model, just as the Quakers conformed in dress, speech, and moral beliefs.

Architectural History as Experienced on Main Street

In the mid-eighteenth century, yards and gardens were becoming more prevalent about town. These had originated with small English side gardens and gradually led to the elaborate formal gardens of the nineteenth century. Quaker beliefs would not allow for flower gardens, dismissing them as too frivolous, but they did allow the kitchen garden, seeing in the vegetable blossoms utility, if not beauty. From these very humble beginnings have grown some of the most beautiful gardens in New England. Hollyhocks, hydrangeas, jasmine, honeysuckles, and roses can be found nearly everywhere in the old town. Indeed, on many of the streets and lanes we can see that some of these "domestic gardens" can scarcely be contained by the fences. The foliage would rather grow through manmade pavements and boundaries, softening and blurring the edges as it reaches out to meet natural counterparts in the heath.

The Quaker restrictions lessened somewhat after the War of 1812, and the later houses reflect those changes. The faces and the layouts of the homes were still informal, but the floor plans were more spacious and not so compartmentalized. The kitchen extension was included right in the original design. Houses were taller and included full basements. Painted clapboards were used for the exteriors, in some cases replacing the earlier utilitarian shingles. Larger panes of glass were readily available for windows. Bolder and more elaborate doorways appeared.

All of these outward embellishments became necessary and important once the houses started being aligned with the streets. The traditional Quaker architecture, like the humble Quaker demeanor, only timidly addressed the world outside. The elaborate homes of the following generation of Nantucket whalemen, however, would not only greet the world, but welcome it inside.

◆ The Turning Point

Classicism in the Colonies, 1720–1850 (111 Main Street; 85 Main Street). Toward the middle of the eighteenth century, nearly everyone on Nantucket was involved in some way in the process of catching whales. The economy stabilized, shifting from an unprofitable agricultural base to a full-blown urban industry.

Whaling and the sea gave Nantucket a cosmopolitan emphasis. At one time isolated by the ocean, the island was now at the crossroads of world trade. Chinese figurines and furniture, European ideas and fashions, all came back to the island via the whaling ship. By the end of the eighteenth century, Nantucket ship masters had become pioneers in the Pacific. They discovered, charted and named

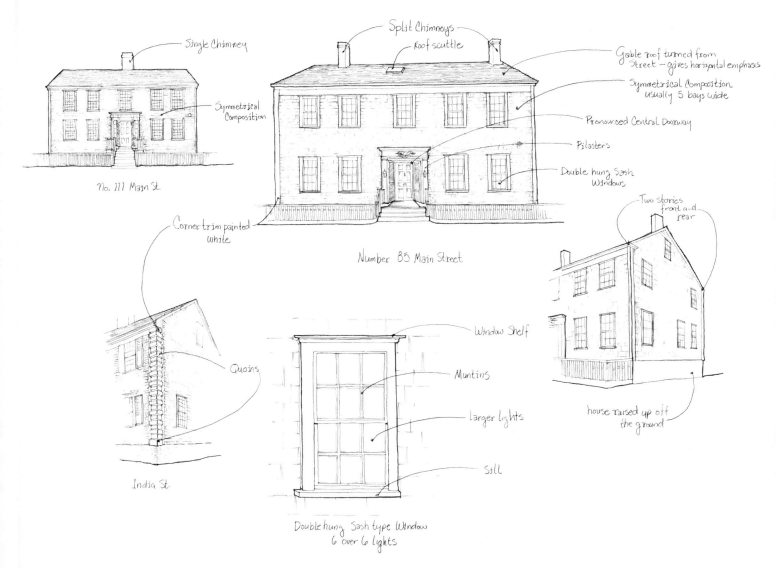

Single Chimney

Symmetrical Composition

No. 111 Main St.

Split Chimneys

Roof scuttle

Gable roof turned from Street – gives horizontal emphasis

Symmetrical Composition usually 5 bays wide

Pronounced Central Doorway

Pilasters

Double hung Sash Windows

Number 85 Main Street

Corner trim painted White

Quoins

India St.

Two stories front and rear

house raised up off the ground

Window Shelf

Muntins

Larger lights

Sill

Double hung Sash type Window 6 over 6 lights

Double House

several Pacific islands. While exploring new territory, the crew of a Nantucket whaler discovered the mutineers from the ship *Bounty* on Pitcairn island, and brought the survivors back to civilization.

The rich merchant class of Nantucket opened its doors to a Europe still steeped heavily in post-Renaissance thought and ideals. It was a time of great enlightenment and an awakening of all the arts and sciences. In the case of architecture, this represented a return to the majestic forms found in classical antiquity.

It was appropriate that this movement began in Italy, where they knew so very little of Gothic spires, and remembered with such emotion the glory that was Rome. The Renaissance architects revived

Architectural History as Experienced on Main Street

an interest in Roman scale, adopting completely the proportioning system called Roman Orders: the use of Doric, Ionic, and Corinthian columns on building facades. The ideas of Italian architects such as Michelangelo, and later Andrea Palladio, were brought to reality in the sixteenth century. From Italy they spread throughout the world. The new form of architecture, however, did not gain a strong foothold in Medieval England until the mid-seventeenth century, consequently arriving on American shores after the turn of the eighteenth century.

In America, public buildings and the houses of the wealthy were the first to show this Renaissance influence. The style began as an imitation of the classical designs of English country houses. (Ironically, Colonists began imitating this English style just at the time they were becoming dissatisfied with British rule.) Builder's guidebooks from England appeared, illustrating this new English style, and American craftsmen copied the stone details in wood. Because the books were readily available, the new styles spread quickly throughout New England. The architects candidly copied Italian ornamentation, door and window details, pilasters, and entry porticoes. Quoins (projecting angles made of wood or stone, sometimes in a contrasting color or texture) were often used to emphasize the corners of a building, making the simple rectangular forms appear heavy, like great Italian stone palaces.

Regardless of whether this style of architecture was correct for New England climate or temperament, the economic conditions were appropriate for an American Renaissance. In effect, we had just stepped out of the Middle Ages. On the mainland this new style was called "Georgian," named for the reign of Kings George I, II, and III (1714–1820). Typical Georgian buildings had a large central hall or passageway, an arrangement that allowed for one large room or two smaller ones on either side of the central hall in both stories. The new interior formality resulted in a symmetrical composition of five window bays on the exterior. Much attention was focused on an elaborate central bay containing the doorway. The central hall required that the traditional central fireplace and chimney be moved to the outside walls. This also allowed the house plan to be further opened up, which admitted more light to the interior. Attention could then be given to a central staircase; until that time staircases had been pushed into a corner or a niche near the entry.

When the Nantucket whalemen visited Philadelphia or Salem, they must have seen these European details translated into American homes. Even so, the Georgian style never really became popular on Nantucket, mostly because it was seen as formal and somewhat pompous. The early whalemen were also Quakers, and the Society of

Friends never would have tolerated such a display of grandness. Instead, they persisted with a sort of double version of the Typical house, with one central fireplace serving both halves. Much like the house at 111 Main Street, it consisted of five bays and was symmetrical in the exterior composition; however, it bore little resemblance to the magnificent Georgians found on the mainland. Even so, with this new modification, the struggle between tradition and innovation began anew.

This was a society that had long gathered around a dominant central hearth. Despite the first timid steps outward, it was still an introverted, nuclear environment. The central fireplace constrained the floor plan, and because it was needed to heat all of the rooms, it was a massive affair. Practicality and function eventually triumphed, as they had once before, when the Typical Nantucket house was developed. The fireplace was split in two and moved to the outside walls, copying ever so conservatively the form of the mainland Georgians. Consequently, the Nantucket house became a symmetrical composition, and more formal in its appearance.

An example of this new innovation can be seen at 85 Main Street. The eastern section of this house was a Typical Nantucket house built around the first quarter of the eighteenth century. The western addition was constructed after the Revolutionary War. A second chimney was added, making the house completely symmetrical. The eagle above the doorway is an American Federal embellishment, a sign symbolizing the birth of a new nation.

Moving the central fireplace to the outside walls was an architectural parallel to a change in society: the shift to extroversion and preoccupation with the world outside. The Quakers suppressed this foreign influence for as long as they possibly could, but even the threat of silence and disassociation could not stop the powerful wheels of fortune. The World's People, as the Quakers had long feared, had now completely taken over.

Federal Style, 1776–1830 (99 Main Street). The eagle above the entry on the house at 85 Main Street is more than mere surface decoration; it was a national symbol. After the Revolutionary War, the collection of independent colonies was fast becoming a nation, and their art and architecture began to reflect this new concept of republic. The infant nation was feeling her own power, economically and politically, rather than that of the British monarchy. Although we had fought for and won our independence from England, the ties of commerce and tradition were still very strong; nevertheless, when the nation needed an architectural style more indicative of her new independent standing in the world, she turned to the European continent.

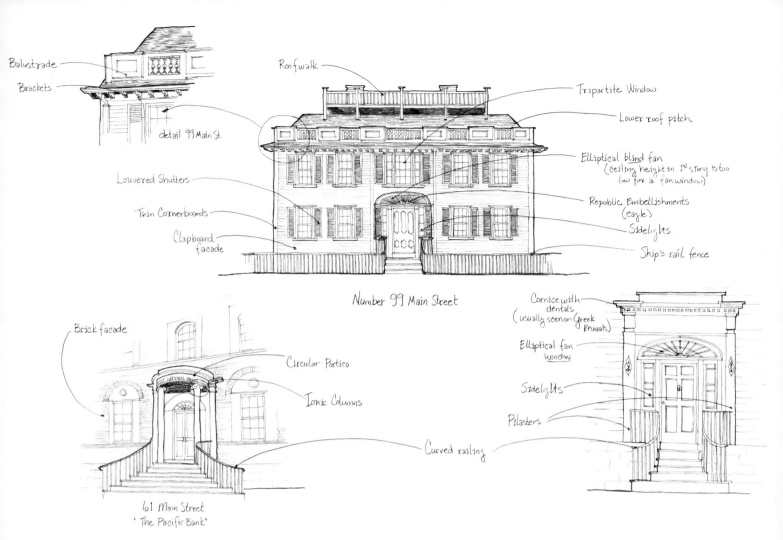

Balustrade

Brackets

detail 99 Main St.

Roofwalk

Tripartite Window

Lower roof pitch

Elliptical blind fan
(ceiling height in 1st story is too
low for a fan window)

Republic Embellishments
(eagle)

Sidelights

Ship's rail fence

Louvered Shutters

Thin Cornerboards

Clapboard
facade

Number 99 Main Street

Brick facade

Circular Portico

Ionic Columns

61 Main Street
" The Pacific Bank"

Cornice with
dentals
(usually seen on Greek
Revivals)

Elliptical fan
window

Sidelights

Pilasters

Curved railing

Federal Style

At the end of the eighteenth century, European architects were occupied with measuring and meticulously drawing the newly uncovered building forms of ancient Rome. Thomas Jefferson, our ambassador to France, drew many parallels between the new American nation and the Roman Empire; furthermore, he completely adopted Roman civic architecture, most notably the temple, for American buildings. Indeed, we have only to recall the image of the United States Capitol building to realize how strongly our national sentiment looked back to Roman antiquity.

A much more formal arrangement in architecture developed as the country itself was evolving from a group of independent states to a nation of common interests. American commerce and trade resumed with a vengeance. Though Nantucket had suffered great losses to her whaling fleet during the Revolution, prosperity and the good life returned to the island afterward. Only a Nantucket captain would have the courage and clout to be the first to sail into London harbor flying the new flag of the United States of America.

The age of the medieval master craftsman was quickly dying out, replaced by a new generation of American architects trained in Europe. Some followed Jefferson and built monumental structures using the Roman Orders and elaborate temple fronts, others continued to base their buildings on models from the English Renaissance. The English Renaissance, though, was moving into its final phase, influenced by the Scottish architect Robert Adam and his brother, James. The Adam brothers reinterpreted the architecture of Andrea Palladio in a very delicate and elegant way, introducing semi-elliptical and circular forms, fanlights over doorways, and tripartite windows. The brothers were perhaps best known, however, for their exquisite interiors, often using grand oval rooms that pushed out into the environment.

Already, on the mainland, the massive central fireplace was being replaced by shallower fireplaces on the end walls. Clapboards were used extensively, and despite the expense were covered with white paint. White buildings were seen as pure and bearing more resemblance to the Classical Roman forms. Architects were beginning to use the lighter and more attenuated elements and orders introduced by the Adam brothers. Doorways became very elaborate, with porticoes or sometimes recessed, causing even more attention to be focused on the center of the facade. The houses had a slightly lower roof pitch, to emulate more closely the flat roofs of the Italian Renaissance. Builders also adapted Italian balustrades and cupolas. Louvered shutters or blinds, common in the hot southern European climate but hardly required in New England, were used without discrimination. This new style of architecture, called Federal, is often seen embellished with decorations from the Republic—eagles and flags.

On Nantucket, whaling in the first half of the nineteenth century created tremendous profits and an even more worldly cosmopolitan attitude. This resulted in an auspicious display of wealth in the houses. The first order of business was to move the chimneys to the outside walls, thereby freeing up the floor plan. Most everything else that followed was ornamental. Many older houses were modified using the exterior motifs of the Federal Style, such as doorways with side lights and elliptical blind fans (or, if the ceiling height in the first story permitted it, fanlights). New houses were somewhat taller by a few feet; in many cases, because of their new elegant proportions they just *seemed* taller.

An excellent example of the American Federal Style translated in a characteristic Nantucket way can be found at 99 Main Street.

Originally, this was a Typical Nantucket house built around 1770 for a shipmaster named Valentine Swain. Later, close to 1830, it was enlarged and embellished for Thomas Macy and his family. It has often been said that this is the most photographed house on the island. Though it is only two and a half stories tall, it projects a restrained elegance and presence to the street unrivaled by earlier structures. It is perfectly symmetrical, with all attention focused on a central doorway surmounted by a blind fan and embellished with a golden eagle. The white clapboards give the house a very clean line, though the lines are broken by the later addition of black shutters. The ship's rail fence, too, helps to give the whole a streamlined horizontal emphasis. Alhough there is a traditional Nantucket roof walk, its rectangular composition is edged by a delicate balustrade reminiscent of Italy.

This new preoccupation with formality and Italian detailing can be seen not only in the mansions along Main Street, but in smaller houses as well. Many can be found in the southern portion of the Fishlots and West Monomoy sections. Also at this time we see the introduction of imposing houses built entirely of brick. Masonry materials were very costly to import to the island; consequently, these houses became a form of status symbol. In less dramatic terms, all of the architecture was becoming very concerned with a new elegant public appearance. It was a full-blown transition from inner-oriented to outer-directed. The height of this Classical trend on Nantucket, however, would be felt in the following generation.

Greek Revival Style, 1820–1860 (1 Pleasant Street). International interest in the Greek and Roman archeological explorations remained strong during the first part of the nineteenth century. English draftsmen had carefully surveyed the Greek ruins and brought back accurately measured drawings of the ancient temples. Pattern books were immediately published with this new material and quickly dispatched across the Atlantic.

In addition, all of the western world's attention was focused on Greece, where the citizens were bitterly fighting for independence from the Turks. Sympathy for the Greek Revolution ran deep in America, where the wounds of the American Revolution were still fresh in the public mind. Moreover, the second expulsion of the British during the War of 1812 had given the Americans a greater sense of national pride. They reasoned that the Classical Greek concept of democracy was very close to the American ideal; furthermore, our laws, philosophy, and educational system were derived from Classical Greece. American architects abandoned their preoccupation with Rome and the fussy details of the Renaissance, and took up the Greek cause. To this extent, the Classical Greek temple became a new national

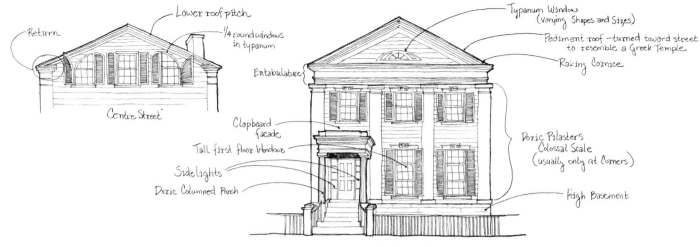

Return

Lower roof pitch

1/4 round windows in typanum

Centre Street

Typanum Window (varying shapes and sizes)

Pediment roof — turned toward street to resemble a Greek Temple

Raking Cornice

Entabulature

Clapboard facade

Tall first floor Windows

Sidelights

Doric Columned Porch

Doric Pilasters Colossal Scale (usually only at corners)

High Basement

Number 1 Pleasant Street

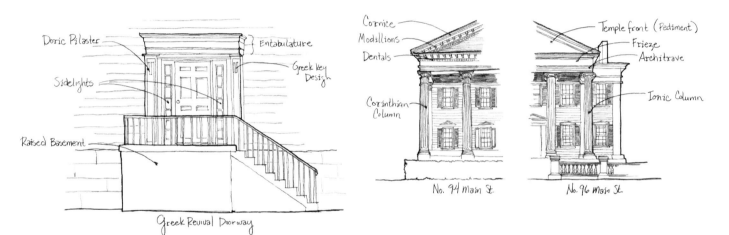

Doric Pilaster

Sidelights

Raised Basement

Entabulature

Greek key Design

Greek Revival Doorway

Cornice

Modillions

Dentals

Corinthian Column

No. 94 Main St.

Temple front (Pediment)

Frieze

Architrave

Ionic Column

No. 96 Main St.

Greek Revival Style

symbol, and it was used as a model for many contemporary American structures.

On Nantucket this national movement coincided with the golden age of whaling, when population and prosperity were at an all-time high. The town was almost wholly formed by then, and many of the streets had been laid with cobbles. The forever elusive prosperity turned out to be short-lived, however, for nearly three hundred buildings, many of the island's oldest structures, were consumed by the Great Fire of 1846. On the positive side, the blaze allowed Nantucketers to rebuild their town center in a modern and contemporary way. In America at the time, the prevailing style was the Greek Revival, and what could be more fitting for a prosperous whaling community than to rebuild in the new national style? In the center of

---

town today, we can see that the majority of buildings are miniature replicas of Classical Greek temples.

To imitate the Greek temple as closely as possible a new structural change was necessary. This time, though, there were very few Quakers around to oppose it. The roof gable was turned around to face the street. In some ways this reorientation worked even better for the narrow in-town lots. The same rectangular floor plan could still be used, and by turning ninety degrees, the narrower side faced the street. Even though the facade was not as wide as in the earlier styles, it had just as much distinction because of its striking similarity to a temple. This new orientation, moreover, demanded a shift in the rectangular plan to orient doors to the front. Some Greek Revivals do have the "front door" on the side, however, thus preserving the earlier traditional arrangement.

A splendid interpretation of the Greek Revival is located just off Main Street at number 1 Pleasant Street. This house was originally built for William Crosby in 1837. Characteristic of the style, the roof pitch is somewhat lower, and a small overhang with return has been added. It has a higher basement to resemble the high temple podiums, and two-story pilasters or flattened columns in the Greek Orders. These pilasters were most often used on the corners of a building to uphold a type of shallow entabulature. On top of this entabulature is the triangular portion of the gable, functioning as a sort of pediment and sometimes containing a unique window form.

Doorways became extremely elaborate in Greek Revival structures, framed by broad pilasters with bases and capitals, much like columns, supporting heavy entabulatures. Often a front porch, or portico, was used to heighten the front door's importance. These outward embellishments gave some of the very humble Quaker houses a larger sense of monumentality and presence than they had ever had before. In a radical departure from the traditional Nantucket house, decoration had finally superseded utility.

The community was completely developed by this time. It was a synthesis of streets, landscape, and architecture working together to create most of the town we see today. Then, as quickly as it had started, the building stopped, and did not resume again for nearly fifty years.

 The Climax

The Romantic Revival 1840–1900. When the sleepy little island reawakened in the late nineteenth century, it was to a com-

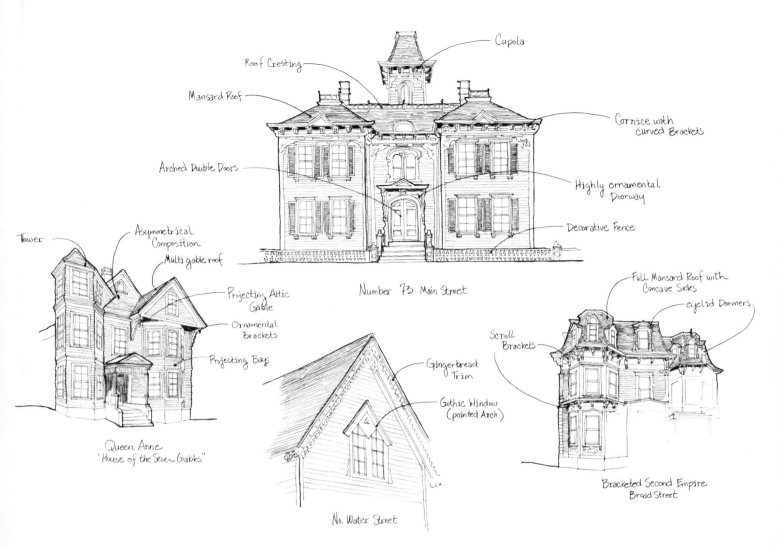

Roof Cresting

Cupola

Mansard Roof

Cornice with
curved Brackets

Arched Double Doors

Highly ornamental
Doorway

Decorative Fence

Number 73 Main Street

Tower

Asymmetrical
Composition

Multi gable roof

Projecting Attic
Gable

Ornamental
Brackets

Projecting Bays

Queen Anne
"House of the Seven Gables"

Gingerbread
Trim

Gothic Window
(pointed Arch)

No. Water Street

Full Mansard Roof with
Concave Sides

eyelid Dormers

Scroll
Brackets

Bracketed Second Empire
Broad Street

Victorian Style

pletely different world: the halcyon days of summer tourism—the
Victorian follies, as some have affectionately termed them. The Industrial Revolution and factory production had created more leisure
time for America's working class. On the other hand, there was
a growing discontent with industrialism; many Americans longed to
return to a simpler way of life. The machine, which was to revitalize
our cities, instead began to choke them, and sent people running
in search of nature and fresh air. A nostalgia for the sea and the
maritime life pervaded the mainland of New England. Seaside resorts were widely sought after, as thousands of Americans fled the
smoke-clogged factory towns during the summer months.

The California Gold Rush and western expansion in the middle of the nineteenth century necessitated a change in building methods as thousands set out across the American prairie. Houses had to be built quickly and cheaply, and balloon-frame structures met the need. This manner of construction, which reached its full realization with the factory production of iron nails, uses thin wooden studs nailed together to form a frame. Soon it completely replaced the earlier technique of connecting heavy structural timbers with mortise-and-tenon joints. Countless cottages from Buffalo to San Francisco were built in this way, sometimes assembled from factory kits shipped west with complete and detailed instructions.

We now had the technology to build great cities—and indeed, in the case of Chicago, we did. The American public, though, still longed for the picturesque. This growing sentiment was manifested in architecture in a movement called Romanticism, which was rooted in a reaction against the earlier formalism and industrial influences. The proverbial pendulum had swung back the other way. As had happened countless times thoughout history, a period of very formal and rigorously correct architecture often was followed by a period in which styles were more informal and relaxed. The architects, seeking to break the shackles of their predecessors, threw themselves into creative experimentation.

Americans pondered their Colonial beginnings, made nostalgic by the American Centennial in 1876. They became preoccupied with romantic literature, such as the tales of King Arthur and his Round Table. Many were completely caught up in the medieval mystique. The first stirrings of a new movement began as a rebirth of Gothic forms. It started superficially, affected by drawings and photographs of castles and the idyllic Gothic ruins of the English countryside. This style brought the return of steeply pitched roofs, sometimes with gingerbread trim and pointed or leaded windows. Although many in America tried to use the Gothic forms for civic architecture, it was deemed more appropriate for churches.

The Gothic Revival Style blossomed during a period of severe depression on Nantucket; consequently, it is seen only in the details of some Nantucket houses, producing a sort of hybrid style. The only fully Gothic Revival structure on the island is the First Congregational Church, called North Tower, at 62 Centre Street.

From these nostalgic beginnings, the period of architecture called Eclecticism, or Victorian, developed. It was named, as Georgian once was, for a British monarch. (Queen Victoria's reign lasted from 1837 to 1901.) The Victorian style was a curious collision of previous styles. Turrets, towers, high-pitched roofs, and curves replaced the Greek and Roman Orders. Color, asymmetry, informality, and gaiety, hardly medieval concepts, came to replace strict formalism as architects again adopted a different kind of ornamentation. This time, though, it was no mere surface decoration; instead, entire houses seemed to be explosions of extroverted forms and styles. Architects broadened their perspectives and looked to the European continent for other forms of inspiration. Consequently, many different styles have evolved out of the Romantic movement.

Italianate Style (76 Main Street). This style was based on the villas and simple farmhouse forms of Italy. Projecting flat roofs and decorative brackets, balconies, and terraces were introduced. The houses were often surmounted by cupolas and square towers. Although very few of these houses were built on Nantucket, a rather modest Italianate can be seen at 76 Main Street.

Second Empire Style (73 Main Street). Napoleon III, seeking to rival his namesake, introduced a new grandness to Paris in the late nineteenth century, and the western world took notice. The movement was popularized by the rebuilding of the Louvre, which received international acclaim. It resulted on this side of the Atlantic in a style of architecture called Second Empire.

Highly monumental and distinctly French, the houses are usually dominated by a heavy mansard roof. This roof style was named for its inventor, seventeenth-century French architect Francois Mansart. Even more than the archaic gambrel, this new roof form permitted a top floor of fully usable space. In addition these houses are sometimes seen with Italian detailing, such as brackets.

At 73 Main Street is a bracketed Second Empire house built for Eliza Barney in 1873. It is capped by a modestly pitched roof. Even though the house was built during the Victorian era, its basic character retains the clear and elegant proportions of the Nantucket houses of earlier times.

East Coast Stick Style. The last period of the Gothic Revival was called the Stick Style. The name is derived from the house's exposed and emphasized structural members. Decorative horizontal, vertical, and diagonal boards—representative of the inner structural system—were placed on the house's exterior. This expression of the inner frame construction was seen as honest and keeping within the basic concept of Gothic half-timbered construction. In many respects it also reflects the elements found in Swiss chalets. In its character, however, the Stick Style has a distinctive medieval look, and represents the final days of the Gothic Revival. A few of these houses can be seen on the bluffs overlooking 'Sconset.

Queen Anne Style (74 Main Street). All of the previous Victorian styles reach their climax in the style known as Queen Anne. The name was borrowed from the reign of Anne, daughter of James II,

which occurred at the turn of the eighteenth century. The style, like Anne's reign, is a curious mixture of Gothic and Renaissance devices. These houses display a multitude of projections and explosions of ornament. Even in the basic exterior covering, straight clapboards were often mixed with scalloped and diamond shingle patterns. This was the ultimate in romanticizing medieval forms— towers, turrets, large porches or verandas, dormers, balconies. Like the formal Greek Revivals before, Queen Anne houses expressed the height of exterior decoration.

At Nantucket a few of these houses were built on the Cliff and Point areas; however, there is a modest example at 74 Main Street.

Shingle Style. The final style in the Victorian era was really a separate movement with a following down to this very day. The American Shingle Style was seen as a revival of Colonial forms and was inspired by seaside resorts where shingle-covered cottages predominated. The houses characteristically have a large encompassing roof with many roof lines, dominant porches, and little or no ornamentation. The entire structure, including porches and columns, moreover, is covered with cedar shingles—hence the name. (Many of these houses can be seen on the 'Sconset bluffs and the Cliff area in town.) The architects of Shingle structures tried to recover the spirit behind the earlier Colonial work. A contemporary version of the American Shingle Style is shown in two small houses on the Pocomo Road. These were designed by the innovative architectural firm of Venturi, Rauch, and Scott-Brown of Philadelphia. With the appearance of these tiny cottages, we have come full circle.

Historical Context

46

There are not as many Victorian structures on Nantucket as can be found on the Vineyard or in parts of the mainland. Although the Quakers had long died out by Victorian times, island residents retained their conservative sentiment and tradition. Here the Victorian structures are seen as explosive moments in the harmonious unity of earlier structures. And because they contrast so sharply with the background of these older structures, they cause us to stop and take notice. In a sense, they seem very animated, like young children showing off in a room full of adults. Or perhaps they can be seen instead as a lasting reminder of a summer romance between Americans and the island of Nantucket.

Architectural styles, like fashions, are cyclical and were often vollyed back and forth between Europe and the New World. The Atlantic Ocean became a sort of vast tennis net. In this manner we influenced one another. When American Colonial architecture had all but exhausted itself, we revived the spirit of European Classicism. This was closely followed by the Romantic Revival, which revitalized the Gothic. Europe would then move into a Renaissance Revival and a Baroque Revival; in America, the skyscraper would be born. Just after World War I, European architects would overthrow the ornamental and introduce a radical new style of architecture that not only acknowledged the machine, but indeed celebrated it. So pervasive was this movement that by 1930 it was universally known as the International Style. Its clean, precise formality has affected generations of Americans and Europeans.

The 1950s and 60s brought new revolutions, both in society and in architecture as more and more Americans found homes in suburbs and housing projects. These concepts, however meaningful on the mainland, are foreign to Nantucket. The little island has attempted to remain, for the most part anyway, true to the Quaker spirit, exhibiting a steadfast indifference to the fashions of the World's People.

2

Basic Observations

Looking at Nantucket's Architecture

◼ Elements and Principles

Just as it is meaningful to know something of the development of architectural styles and the context out of which they grew, it is also important when looking at buildings to understand that the three-dimensional realization of the style is indeed an artistic composition. These stylistic compositions, like different languages, have separate vocabularies. Architectural vocabularies are made up of such elements as *line, form, color,* and *texture,* and are governed by the principles of *rhythm, balance, proportion,* and *scale.* Some of these concepts might entirely overtake a composition, as color and asymmetrical balance often dominated the houses of the Victorian era. Other elements and principles within the same style are secondary and hardly noticeable—for instance, the subtle horizontal rhythm created by the clapboard joints, or the texture produced by the pattern of shingles. Just as the artful manipulation of words and grammar composes different stories, these elements and principles create for us different architectural styles.

Before we learn a new language, we usually try to gather something of its *character,* or its essence. Architectural character is very much like an individual's basic personality, and, like moods, character can change with the light and the season. In some buildings, like certain people, their basic character is disguised beneath layers of facades, or styles, but sooner or later their true essence will usually become apparent.

The Nantucket personality is a maritime character. Although it is trim and shipshape, it is also weathered, craggy, and gray. Like a treasured old aunt, a Nantucket house has a multitude of stories to tell. All of the island structures are of this same basic character, despite their stylistic differences. In many ways, the houses can be seen together as a grand family. Each generation is a little more sophisticated than the last, but all of them have grown from the same basic roots.

Words such as "personality" and "family" used in reference to architecture may raise a few eyebrows. Later, when I describe the "dialogues" between buildings, eyebrows might lift higher still, so perhaps I should introduce the concept here, before going on to describe specific Nantucket neighborhoods.

Not long ago, during an intense critique, a student in my second-year design studio threw a mild tantrum, exclaiming: "You architects always say that this or that building is 'talking' with another one, or that there is a 'dialogue' or tension between parts. I have even heard you say that buildings 'sing'! Or that they do *not* speak to each other at all. What does it mean, anyway? Architects never bother to explain it." He had a point: architects and planners do talk this way, leaving non-architects looking perplexed, as if they had missed the point of an in-joke. I have even heard some of my colleagues say that a building "scoffs at its surroundings" or "sneers" or "smiles." To the best of my knowledge, no one has yet attempted a written definition of these purely sensory episodes and metaphors, but I will take the plunge by offering the following "glossary."

Talks: This occurs when two or more buildings complement one another through their forms, colors, textures, or rhythms—especially through their *forms*. For example, in a pair of buildings, one seems to push forward, the other to recede. From a different viewpoint, however, the two buildings can switch characters; the more modest one becomes the new center of attention, while the originally more "animated" building seems to become more subdued. They work well together as a team. With buildings, as with human beings, the most successful relationships usually include an element of give-and-take.

Sings: This happens when all the buildings or all the parts of one building are in harmony with one another, showing the same rhythm, the same scale, etc. Each element is necessary in the overall arrangement, just as every member is necessary in an orchestra. In harmonious groupings, the removal of even one building would disturb the whole composition—imagine Beethoven's Fifth Symphony without the horns.

Does not speak: Often this happens when buildings are planned with no regard for the surrounding buildings or landscape. Sometimes new buildings are designed to be the star; they seem to have been planned without regard to the older buildings' scale, rhythm, and forms. The landscape is bulldozed, and the new structure overshadows everything else in order to establish its position. In this case, no one "talks"; everyone isdisturbed and uncomfortable. A comparable phenomenon happens in business all the time, when one company forcibly takes over another.

In attempting to define these architectural concepts I have inevitably explained one set of metaphors with yet other metaphors, but there seems to be no better way to explain such intangible (and individualistic) impressions on paper. They are so much better explained in person and on the spot. I can only suggest that you let your own experience of Nantucket—and of other places and architecture in general—be both sensory and analytical. Imagine each building to be like a person, each cluster of houses like a group of individuals, and soon you will begin to understand when conversations come up in the environment.

Looking at architecture across water, with so many light reflections, causes it to appear dreamlike, or even without depth. The white outlining on Nantucket buildings makes each one stand apart and distinct from the others surrounding it; moreover, the bold outlining gives the building a mass that the light reflections tend to diminish. All of architecture is made up of lines; on Nantucket, these lines are emphasized. They describe the edges and give shape to the form. At times they can be moody. Some lines are hard and angular, as are those composing the older Quaker structures. They are as unyielding as the Quakers were in their beliefs. We call these lines severe. Others are curved and playful, such as those defining the portico on the Pacific Bank building, and still other lines can be elegant like the ones defining the great Classical-inspired whaling mansions on Main Street.

On Nantucket, windows, doors, and edges of the facade are given distinction. This outlining trim around doorways and windows was originally used, as were shingles and clapboards, to seal the raw edges against the wind and rain; the early housewrights were not really concerned with beauty at all. Simple shapes can be made to look grander and heavier by emphasizing the basic lines or edges. Carved wooden quoins, for example, placed on the corners of a building cause it to appear heavier than its neighbors.

Architecture is composed of planes, the predominant ones being vertical (walls) and horizontal (floors and roofs). A brief stroll down Main Street reveals that on Nantucket the planes work together in a variety of ways depending on the time and place of their construction. Architectural walls might have a completely different meaning if we were to view them in the abstract; that is, as the end result of a struggle between the interior forces—family needs, values, concerns—pushing out and the exterior forces—society, environment, culture—pushing in. In this way, walls control the relationship between the inside of the house and the outside world. The Quakers sought to keep the world at bay. Their walls formed straight lines, dramatically separating the inside from the outside and allowing communication only through small windows and modest doorways. The walls of the whaling captains' houses, on the other hand, pushed out *into* the environment with lavish porches or porticoes and large windows. These houses seem to be welcoming the world inside. In addition, the same walls that push or pull our interiors define the street's edge and give it a special character.

On Nantucket we can see a multitude of inside-to-outside relationships translated through walls. Probably the most compelling relationship is seen when a house addresses the water. The wall planes tend to push out and over the water with balconies and terraces, sometimes steps. This indicates a pleasant give-and-take dialogue with the sea. Rarely do we notice a house set directly on the water's edge that does not reach out to the sea in some meaningful way.

Interesting relationships can also be seen between architecture and the sky. These are translated through the lines composing the roof. Early houses reached up high into the sky with their steep peaks, as if to communicate with the heavens. In later houses the roof pitch was dropped, becoming almost flat, silent, like those resting above the Classical whaling captain's mansions. The only outward sign of a relationship with the sky was the roof walks, though these had their spiritual eyes turned not toward heaven but out to sea.

When all of a structure's walls or planes come together, they create form. On Nantucket, each house can be broken down into the simple shapes of square, rectangle, and triangle, and each style has used these basic forms in distinctly different ways. However, they all have one thing in common: they are additive compositions, meaning that one starts with one solid form and adds others to it. As mentioned before, on Nantucket these additions are called warts.

A multitude of similar forms might indicate the intensity of a certain culture; for instance, the great number of Typical Nantucket houses built between 1750 and 1820 reveals the vast number of Friends in Nantucket society. These forms sit at attention, stoically facing one another across a street. They call to mind, perhaps, a solemn moment from a Quaker meeting.

Other forms press forward into our space, soliciting a response. These are forms representative of an extroverted world, a

world of wealth and cosmopolitan ideals. Curved forms are especially effective in this way. The portico of the Pacific Bank building or the brick shop adjacent to it, with its swelling front walls, reach out and invite us inside. Moreover, solid forms create void spaces between them, and these become the streets, lanes and public squares.

Forms can also have color and texture. These elements are enhanced by the quality of light during different times of the day and throughout the seasons. When the island is overcast, everything looks gray and even the rough texture of the shingles blurs; hence Nantucket's affectionate nickname, "the little gray lady out to sea." Most all of the shingle-covered structures have been allowed to weather gray. The use of color on a building will affect our depth perception and the building's visual weight. White-painted clapboard houses stand out. They strike us as being somewhat lighter and more delicate than their dark-shingled or brick neighbors. Yellow, blue, and red buildings similarly distinguish themselves, calling for our

Looking at Nantucket's Architecture

attention. The cooler colors tend to recede, while the warmer ones appear to press forward. Even when different colored houses sit directly on the street's edge, our eye will perceive a subtle shifting back and forth.

The natural environment changes hues many times throughout the year, providing us with an intense sensory experience. It is appropriate that the majority of buildings on Nantucket remain neutral in color, for they make a wonderful backdrop for the seasonal natural colors. If all of the buildings were painted, we can imagine that the effect would be overwhelming and chaotic, and nature would not seem nearly as dramatic.

Nantucket is about texture—indeed, it is everywhere we turn. Certainly it is apparent in nature, but it can also be seen in architecture. A building's surface appearance, or texture, also helps us to judge the character and weightiness of the structure. Shingles or bricks not only cause a building to appear warmer, but also heavier than it's smoother clapboarded neighbors. In addition, textured materials are more likely to reveal their aging process. Wood ages well; like a face, it shows the lines of its history. The cedar shingles change from a warm white to a yellow-ochre when first put up, to shades of gray when exposed to weather, and particularly the salt air. Everywhere about the town we see shingles and the passage of time. Very little on Nantucket is perfectly smooth or gives the slick appearance of being machine made. Nearly everything reveals that it has been cut by hand from wood.

Contrasts dominate the island: the smooth clapboards in contrast to rough shingles, the sleek shapes of boats' hulls in contrast to the pleasant irregularity of the buildings' facades. Even the floor planes are quite varied: in addition to the conventional asphalt, we see brick, cobble, clamshell, sand, and grass surfaces. Ceiling planes provide a multitude of textures defined by overhanging foliage; diversity is created by the different shapes of trees and

Basic Observations

Looking at Nantucket's Architecture

leaves. Almost all of the vertical surfaces are textured: brick, shingle, clapboard, pickets, trees. The contrast and layering of these materials create a Nantucket collage impossible to duplicate even in photographs: foliage and wildflowers, sand, nautical textures of chains, ropes, riggings, lobster traps, rusted hulls, shiny ships—all coexisting peacefully with three centuries of American architecture.

When the basic elements of line, form, color, and texture repeat over and over in architecture, we call this principle *rhythm*. The universal rhythms of nature are many, and they represent the very essence of being alive. Moving, breathing, laughing, and dancing all involve rhythm to a certain degree, although we usually associate rhythm with music and the beat of a drum marking time. The German philosopher Johann von Goethe was so taken with architecture that he described it as frozen music. Despite his moving analogy, though, rhythm in architecture is still not so easily defined. In music, it is the result of change, with the best rhythms providing smooth changes, like melodies blending into one another, creating movement and countermovement.

In architecture, too, we can see regular or harmonic reoccurrences of elements in the composition. In individual pieces, it is the window rhythm that we usually notice first. On Nantucket, window sizes were standardized and their arrangement on the facade was also duplicated over and over. On a Typical Nantucket house we can see a rhythm of window, window, door, window, or 1-2-**3**-4, 1-2-**3**-4. What dance step is this? In the later styles, the number of window bays sometimes increased to five, but the window size remained nearly the same. As we look down the tiny streets we notice that the standard window openings provide a continuous harmony for the movement and countermovement of the forms.

Even roof walks can establish a peculiar rhythm along the street. Doors, too, display a different rhythm because they are usually the only piece of trim painted a contrasting color. A street's rhythm can be fast or slow. When there is an abundance of vegetation, the rhythm tends to be slower, moving around and absorbing the foliage. It is faster where there are repetitive houses and stoops, as seen, for instance, in the splendid choreography of facades on India Street. Nantucket streets are often stitched together by the uniformity of white picket fences, connecting facade to facade and serving as the horizontal lines of the musical score.

Most all of architecture is visually balanced in some manner, and two types predominate, asymmetrical and symmetrical. These provide an ordering method for the entire composition. Conceptually, *balance* in architecture often has been compared to two pairs of scales. The first scale has equal arms holding equal-sized weights; in

Balance

Asymmetrical   Symmetrical

other words, the distribution is equal on both sides of the center. This is called symmetrical balance. The second scale is more complex, it can be imagined as having unequal arms, with the longer arm supporting a smaller mass and the shorter arm supporting a larger mass. Because of their position relative to the pivot, the scale balances. This is called asymmetrical balance. When a composition is balanced symmetrically it is seen as more formal and stable, or static. On the other hand, when a building is arranged asymmetrically it is said to be more casual. Sometimes an asymmetrical composition is more interesting, as our eyes and brain must work harder to perceive the order in the composition.

On Nantucket, symmetry corresponded with wealth. Most of the houses of the prosperous whaling captains are large rectangles with their elements equally balanced about an elaborate central doorway. Asymmetrical balance was reserved for the houses of the Quakers, and later during the more casual resort architecture of the Victorian era.

The architectural principle of proportion is complex and based on a mathematical ratio. It can be the building's height to width ratio. Nantucket house proportions are typically 2:3 or 3:4. The overall visual proportion is also based on the ratio of parts to the whole. House parts, such as windows, doors, columns, or porticoes are judged to be in proportion to the entire house form.

Throughout history, each culture has derived its own proportioning systems. Pythagoras, an ancient Greek mathematician, discovered a ratio that he felt to be the most harmonious. He claimed that if a line is divided such that the shorter segment is proportionate to the larger segment in the same way that the larger segment is proportionate to the whole, an entire set of like proportions can be derived. Algebraically, this can be expressed as $a/b = b/a{+}b$. The ratio

Asymmetrical ducks. Asymmetry is often more pleasing to the eye than symmetry, for the mind is challenged to find the order.

is constant and equals about five parts to eight parts, or $5/8$, or .625. The ancient Greeks found that the human body was also proportioned in this manner. They reasoned that the ratio was the most divine, and employed it in the proportioning of their temples. When a and b define the sides of a rectangle, the proportion can easily be applied to architecture. This is called the Golden Section, or the Golden Rectangle.

Although the Nantucket craftsmen were possibly ignorant of Pythagoras' ancient theory, many of the later Nantucket houses comprising five bays have the proportion of width to height corresponding to the Golden Section. Although they did not know the mathematical ratio, the builders understood visually that these proportions created the most elegant forms. This ideal proportion is in common use even today. The shapes of credit cards, driver's licenses, and standardized paper sheets, for example, are all based on this Golden Section. If we hold a credit card in front of the house at 99 Main Street, the two rectangles are exactly proportionate to one another.

The Greeks and Romans also used proportioning devices termed *Orders*. These were based on the use of certain structural columns. The Greek Orders comprised Doric and Ionic columns; the Roman Orders also allowed Doric and Ionic, and included a third, the Corinthian column. The names refer to the appearance of the top part of the column, or its capital. On a Classical temple, the smallest unit of measurement was the diameter of a column at its base. From this basic module, all of the dimensions of the structure were derived. In other words, the entire building might be so many modules wide and

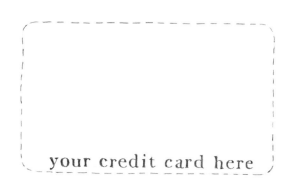

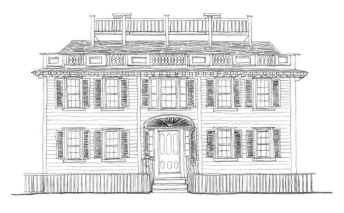

99 Main

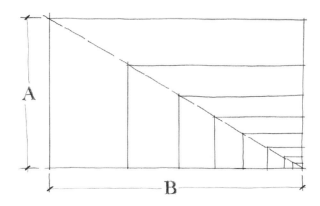

The Golden Section

so many modules high with each and every part proportionate to the basic module. In this way, all of the parts seem to be in harmony with one another.

The Roman Orders was the proportioning system revitalized during the Renaissance. It was the same system that Thomas Jefferson adopted in the late eighteenth century for the proportioning of American buildings. Many Classic Revival structures with their columned fronts and porticoes have been proportioned in this manner.

Although proportion corresponds to a mathematical ratio, scale refers to the way we perceive the size of something. We intuit the size of a building by comparing it with something else, usually something in which the size is known. It is easiest to compare that unknown size either with the things around it, or with ourselves. When a building's parts and its whole have dimensions relating to the human body, we say that the building is human scale.

For generations the American craftsman used his own body as a measuring device for building; thus the terms *ell* (the length

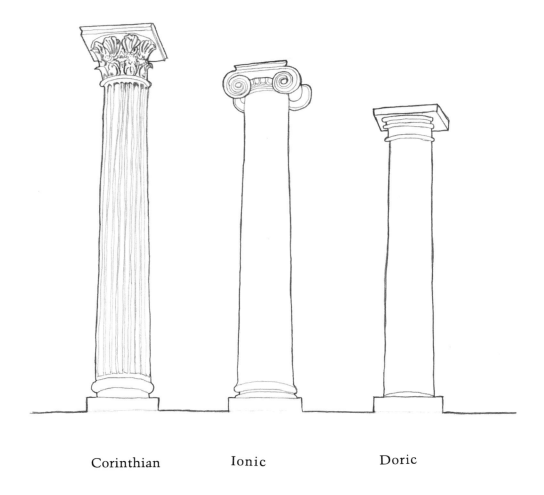

Corinthian   Ionic   Doric

The Orders

from one's elbow to the finger tip), *fathom* (the breadth of one's outstretched arms), *foot* (direct meaning), and *inch* (the breadth of one's thumb.) These were universally accepted and applied. For example, three ells equaled one fathom, and twelve inches, a foot. Though we seldom refer anymore to ells or fathoms, inches and feet are still in common use despite the persistence of the scientific community to adopt the metric system.

     Bricks and shingles were originally scaled to human hands and for the ease of manual construction. We can determine the height of a particular building by counting how many shingles or bricks tall it is, then multiplying by the width or double the width of one's hand. Buildings that are human-scaled encourage interaction with the environment, they make us feel as if human beings, rather than machines, are in control. They are comfortable. Most all of the structures on Nantucket were scaled to human dimensions.

We accept a larger, or a monumental, scale in public buildings. This is set not by human dimensions but instead by a column size or by other individual elements. When a column rises two stories, it is said to be colossal, or of the monumental scale. Classical Revival structures, with their ornamentation adapted from stone pattern books, are often seen as grand in size. The temples after which they were modeled were massive structures, scaled more appropriately for gods than humans. Monumental scale becomes even more effective when seen in the context of human-scaled houses. There is a Typical Nantucket house on Hussey Street with a modern studio window cut into the front facade. Although this window fulfills the functional concern of capturing important north light, the huge opening dwarfs the tiny house and throws its composition out of scale.

Public buildings in a smaller residential area also present this same monumentality. The Methodist Church on Centre Street, with its majestic two-story portico, is not that much taller than the surrounding buildings; however, the overscaled columns make it appear massive. The Atheneum, on Federal Street, displays two scales, the two-story temple portico is of the monumental scale, proportionate to the entire building; the actual doors through which we enter, though, are scaled for human beings. The Pacific Club is a three-and-a-half-story building, but the bricks give it a warm human feeling; moreover, the horizontal brick stringcourses identify the stories and bring it down to human scale.

Streets, too, have scale. Nantucket streets were originally planned for the horse and buggy and for pedestrians. Today, the automobile scarcely seems at home on these old, narrow lanes. A delivery truck looks hopelessly out of scale, like an adult in a doll's house.

When elements and principles work together to give a harmonic appearance, we say that the building has *order*. Entire communities, like Nantucket, can show order. It is created first by a homogeneous character and secondarily by uniformity: repetitive forms, scales, colors, even roof pitches help to create a carefully ordered and rhythmic environment. The preponderance of shingled houses, all proportionate to one another, sets the rhythm, order, and character of the old town.

Even though sameness creates an ordered environment, it is the very juxtaposition and interplay of a diversity of styles that helps to make Nantucket Town so vital. Buildings, like the people within a community, can be different in personality and appearance. In every society we have the conformists, the leaders, the artists, and the poets. In buildings, too, we have rebels. When they act in concert with one another, though, the effect can be overwhelming, producing a rich community complete with meaningful dialogue and playful relationships.

Looking at Nantucket Town

⬠ Physical Events

Nantucket Town creates one face for visitors arriving by sea and a completely different one for those who arrive by land. To the person arriving by sea, the entire town is revealed in a single magnificent panorama. It is only when we disembark that we discover the small scale. Similarly, if we chance to fly to the island and arrive by auto from the airport, Nantucket reveals herself to us slowly; her intricacies and special places evolve along the route, one at a time. After we pass through what seems to be an endless forest of scrub oaks, one small shingled cottage appears at last, then two, then six. Soon, like a crowd of people, they line the approach to town. As we turn the bend, the golden lantern of South Tower comes into view and welcomes us. We slip quietly into town through the back door. The town's elaborate front entry is the harbor, exploding with lines, flags, and wharves.

For those of us who chance to arrive in late September, when the crowds have disappeared and the days are growing noticeably shorter, Nantucket projects a special quality, a charm that she reserves for her residents alone. The island community, like most memorable cities, is a grand composition, a complex organization; however, it is never fully created. Each culture, for generations, has left something of itself behind in the architecture and the town.

When buildings seem to respond to each other and to the needs of people, neighborhoods are born. In large cities, such as New York or Boston, we call these harmonious groupings *districts*, or *regions*. The Village in Manhattan or the North End in Boston are such districts, always unique in character. Nantucket Town is not large enough or ethnically diverse enough to produce a district the size of

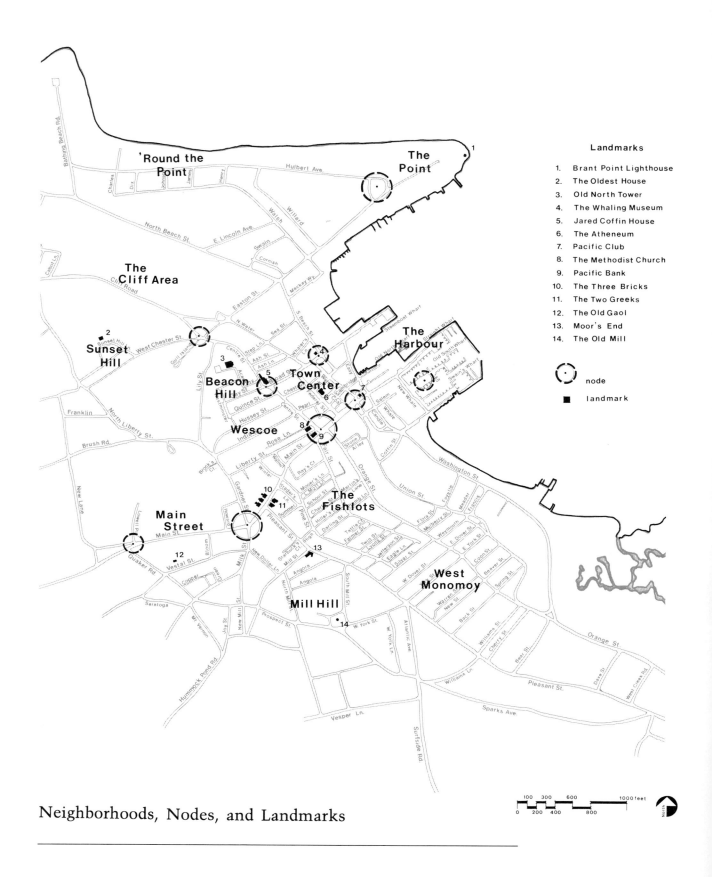

Landmarks

1. Brant Point Lighthouse
2. The Oldest House
3. Old North Tower
4. The Whaling Museum
5. Jared Coffin House
6. The Atheneum
7. Pacific Club
8. The Methodist Church
9. Pacific Bank
10. The Three Bricks
11. The Two Greeks
12. The Old Gaol
13. Moor's End
14. The Old Mill

node

landmark

Neighborhoods, Nodes, and Landmarks

Basic Observations

66

those in a great metropolis. A small town does have its individual neighborhoods, though. Groups of buildings that form neighborhoods have a homogeneous character different from that of other areas. In addition to their individual ethnic, social, political, and economic makeups, neighborhoods often are defined by physical events called *edge* or *boundary, gateway, path, gathering node,* and *landmark.*[5]

Neighborhoods often have a continuous harmony or rhythm composed of styles, materials, forms, or topography. In any individual neighborhood, moreover, the more distinct the identifying characteristics, the stronger the unit or district becomes. The Harbor presents a unique area. This neighborhood's very proximity to the water dictates its materials, forms, and character. The central part of Nantucket, adjacent to the Harbor, was rebuilt after the Great Fire. It contains commercial buildings composed almost exclusively in the Greek Revival style. In this neighborhood there is a continuity communicated by function, style, and scale. The same can be said for the Cliff and Point areas. These were developed in the beginning days of summer tourism, and therefore the architectural styles are reminiscent of the Romantic era and later. Materials and textures are similar to the other neighborhoods, although the scale and rhythm are completely different. A change in topography, too, sometimes creates a different neighborhood pattern, as can be seen on Beacon and Sunset Hills.

The island has an endless array of districts from long ago. The colorful old names such as Chicken Hill, Egypt, New Guinea, and Cambridge are nearly extinct by now, remembered only by a few older residents. Some of the Indian names for the small outlying communities have persisted over the years, though: Siasconset (called 'Sconset), Madaket and Quidnet, to name a few. Their very remoteness has created some small separate districts—for instance Eel Point, Great Point, and Coatue.

Usually districts and neighborhoods are contained in some manner by a boundary. The most memorable neighborhoods have a definite edge, although this edge is not necessarily as severe or permanent as a wall. The Quanaty Bank, which runs above Union Street, provided a natural boundary for the Fishlots division. Some of the most memorable edges on the island involve the junction of land and water. The dominant edge of the Great Harbor gives Nantucket Town its definition, though it is blurred by the preponderance of wharves. Revealed on this small island are a diversity of coastlines: the bluffs at Sankaty Head and 'Sconset present an ever-changing face of sand and clay and rock; soft dune areas define the North Shore and Dionis; and endless flats merge Madaket, Wauwinet, and Quidnet with the sea.

Individual pieces of architecture respond to these natural water boundaries with their own edges composed of walls, terraces, and stairways, just as the town addresses these natural edges with piers, wharves and fences. Other man-made edges can be streets, paths, or even railroad tracks. Like picket fences, edges can be uniting seams, joining one neighborhood with another. Anything, visible or invisible, that marks the spot where different natural or constructed elements touch one another, could be called an edge.

Most all neighborhoods or districts have a main entry point, this could be termed a gateway. It does not have to be a physical gateway; usually it is only a symbolic one, like the Harbor area, which serves as the point of entry to the whole of Nantucket Town. Occasionally two monumental buildings stand close to one another on a street, functioning as a ceremonial gate, as the Two Greeks stand to welcome us onto Pleasant Street and the southern part of town. A monument in the middle of the street can signify transition into another area. The Civil War Monument marks the end of Main Street in town, and the beginning of Upper Main Street, which leads out into the country. It also marks both the beginning of another area surrounding Milk Street to the south and the beginning of Gardner Street, the edge that separates the original Wescoe Acres from the part of town to the west. Bridges, too, form gateways of a sort. The bridge in 'Sconset forms the gateway to the beach, and as we walk across or under it we cannot help but feel a sense of ceremony. Gateways, like doorways, give us a sense of anticipation; they signal a change and a beginning. At gateways we physically or symbolically leave one sequence and move into another.

Streets and paths dictate how we move through an environment. They function very much like the circulatory system in the human form. Each road gives life to the surrounding body of architecture. Principal roads often have been likened to spines. Main Street is the most important spine in Nantucket Town, linking north and south, or the old and new parts of the community. Roads can be ordering devices for entire cities. A characteristic radial street plan defines Washington D.C. The gridiron street systems of New York and Los Angeles provide diverse rhythms uniquely adapted for the automobile. Nantucket's street system is much like the tangled net of old streets that form the North End in Boston. It grew naturally from the seventeenth- and eighteenth-century lot line divisions and moved with the rolling topography of the land.

In days gone by, each road had a distinct character and function. Orange and Main streets were once home to over one hundred sea captains. Many streets were originally named for what could be found along their edges, such as Fair Street, Milk Street, Church Lane, and Mill Street. We can only guess what could be found on

Tattle Court or Easy Street. India Street got its name from a visitor's observation that everyone on that street seemed to live in such ease and comfort.

Like architecture, streets have scale. Some, such as Main, Broad, and Centre, were widened; the majority, however, display the scale for which they were created. Nantucket roads were built for simple purposes and wagon transportation. Some of the most delightful paths on the island are those narrow, curving rural lanes leading out of the main town. Their forms roll along, their edges dense with pines, and there is little visible development. They follow the island's natural terrain, rising, dipping and zig-zagging around the gentle hills. The passing glimpses of ocean or pond, bog or moor, contrast sharply with the views found in town, and through this contrast they delight us. Each memorable path forms the stage for the interplay of people, architecture, and nature.

Where there is an intersection in a path, one can feel a heightening of energy. A decision must be made: Do I turn left? Continue straight ahead? Consequently, we become more *aware* of our surroundings as we approach this part of the path. People tend to pause or gather at these spots. At places where the surroundings are set back further from the roadway, the space is called a node (or a square or a courtyard, to use the more common terms). In America these originated with the central common around which the village was built. Influenced by European traditions, some American commons have been developed into grand city squares much like Rockefeller Plaza in New York or Copley Square in Boston. In Nantucket, though, the public squares have remained modest. Perhaps the most dominant is the market square formed by Lower Main Street.

Where the level of activity and decision-making is high, a node requires more space. This can be seen at the intersection of many streets or paths. Main Street Square displays this quality. To carry this further, the entire length of Main Street can be seen as a vital linear node connecting the busy harbor area with the remainder of town. Where the level of energy is lower, the node can be a much more intimate space, as in the crossing of two footpaths, or as experienced in Pump Square in 'Sconset. Squares and courtyards most often have personalities. Main Street is like a large traffic center, dispatching people and automobiles elsewhere, it is an extroverted node. The shady courtyard in the center of Old South Wharf, however, draws people to it in the summertime, and is rather introverted in its space.

These nodes are really outdoor rooms with streets forming the doorways. They can also be centers of passive activity, such as the spaces found in front of major buildings or churches where people tend to gather. The more consistent the shape of the outdoor area and the exterior elevations of the architecture enveloping the space, the more compelling the image of an outdoor room. Within the most delightful of these "rooms" are found fountains, benches, monuments, and trees. These compare to the familiar furniture in a cherished indoor room.

When the surrounding architecture responds sympathetically to the character and level of energy, then the gathering node becomes even stronger, and when a landmark is placed within the node or adjacent to the node, the space becomes most vital.

Landmark is a nautical term. In days gone by, many physical events "marked the land" for ships to steer toward or lay their courses by. Today, landmarks form a network over entire towns, marking strategic points and letting us know where we are in the environment by their reference. How much joy the whaling crews must have felt when they rounded the Point after three years at sea and beheld the reassuring steeples of Old South Tower and Old North Tower peeking through the fog. They were signs that all was well in Nantucket Town.

When we first encounter an unknown environment, it is the landmarks that we come to know first. They are the wayfinders. Just as a lighthouse—a dramatic form of landmark—guides ships, either by beckoning them home or warning of dangerous shoals, a landmark in the community gives us reference for where we are at any given moment. Once we choose to know the environment more closely, we begin to orient ourselves by them. If we get to know the environment intimately, as we would by living in it, we create our own wayfinders.

There are four basic types of landmarks. Some, such as lighthouses or towers, have *spatial prominence* and are visible from many locations. Others display *contextual differences;* they provide contrast by differing from their backgrounds in style, function, materials, or scale. Some have *historical or cultural significance,* providing a connection to the history of the civilization that built them, while others have an individual or *personal attachment* for us.

Often landmarks fall into more than one of these categories; this reinforces the strength of the individual landmark. South Tower, in the center of town, is one of these. We can always orient ourselves by standing back and looking up to find it marking Main Street square and the intersection of Orange Street. In addition to having spatial prominence, it contrasts sharply with the scale of the residential neighborhood. It has historical significance for the town, and it holds a personal meaning for many Nantucketers.

Landmarks are not always something built. Ponds and hills can be landmarks or wayfinders in the wild. A particular panorama or bench where you can sit and enjoy a special view can be a landmark. It could be a gnarled tree that marks a favorite path, or even the

counter in the drug store that has been there since the community began. Even the houses of special people can become landmarks. We make up our own personal set of landmarks depending on our degree of closeness with the environment. As Hansel and Gretel learned when they scattered the precious bread crumbs, though, landmarks are only viable as wayfinders if they endure over time.

Imagine cityscapes to be like mindscapes. If we could travel back in time, through the special hills and valleys of the mind's landscape, we would find the nodes, the landmarks, and the edges of our lives: nodes where we had choices to make, landmark events that persist even to this very day in our memory, and edges over which we have often tripped in a daydream. A city's physical events, like life's events, are carefully built up over time. If they are taken separately, they remain only momentary physical events. It is when we begin to see the gateways, the nodes coexisting with the landmarks, and the paths and edges blending into neighborhoods, that we realize the true meaning of the word *community*. It ceases to be an odd collection of architecture and becomes instead a memorable place in time and space.

3

The Nantucket Experience

Indian summer harvest.

In the Neighborhoods

Since the beginning of time, people have dreamed of ideal places, temporary escapes, and visions of faraway lands. These images reach out, tempting us away from the reality of cities and suburbs. Visions sometimes change into journeys, or voyages to relive our past and contemplate our future. These special journeys take place occasionally only in the mind with a good book, in the friendly atmosphere of an overstuffed chair. Other journeys happen purely by accident, when we chance to hear an old wooden door slam or see a chair rocking on a porch with no one else around or smell a pie that has just come out of the oven. At each encounter we imagine a hundred things: conversations, smells, delights, fights, births, deaths. Instantly we are transported back in time, an entire mental matrix arises and envelops us for a short while. The bravest travelers among us move past the images and actually seek out and find special places in time.

Nantucket is about time. The intricate village complexities and the ever-changing expanse of nature are visible reminders of the passage of time. The island wears her past not like shiny medals but rather like a comfortable old cloak, stitched together by worn cobbles, now-silent wharves and roof walks, sparkling balustrades and stoops; in each, the details have been embroidered by the lines of time. The town presents us with an historic process larger than our immediate lives. It provides an assurance that life goes on, and change inevitably occurs, and that gives us a certain sense of security. There is nothing more poignant that a resort town in the still of winter, nothing as lonely as a rusted barbecue in January, yet at the same time, these images are filled with dormant expectations, for warmth, activity, and change nearly always follow the spring.

On Nantucket the architecture seems antique and permanent, only nature is allowed to change. The splendid heath turns different colors and textures throughout the year; new daffodils and crocuses open each spring beside a three-hundred-year-old house, illustrating for us the wonderful contradiction of old and new, and the peaceful coexistence of both. The houses on Nantucket may appear to remain the same, but their very spirit changes with the seasons. They almost seem to dance in the summer months, wearing window boxes filled with brightly colored flowers, smelling of new paint, and sporting a few new shingles among the weathered gray ones. In January, the same house is quiet. Its window boxes have been removed; only the hooks and a barely discernible outline remain. Storm windows have been carefully put up, and paint is beginning to peel in the salt air. Every time we confront a Nantucket house we find ourselves caught up in a dialogue, eavesdropping on a conversation, for concealed within each house, as within each person, lies at least one story worthy of a novel.

Nantucket is an intricate choreography of architecture and nature, displaying at once our past and our present, barely whispering our future. It gives us a sense of living history to walk down a street that our forefathers trod every day, to ponder a place or a house that stood not only through two World Wars, but during the American Revolution and Civil War as well. Certain special images evoke in us an awakened consciousness of a particular historical period. Who built that house? What child carved those initials into that tree? What did he become: a pauper, a statesman, a sailor, an artist? Whose history is concealed within those walls? These images can help to strengthen our own identity, and as well our sense of community as Americans. Our ancestors are no longer alive to tell us stories, so their environment must.

The vegetable carts on Main Street are a reminder of long ago, of a simpler time, when vegetables and flowers were not packaged in cellophane and marked neatly with a mute price tag. The carts take us back to a time when one's daily shopping included an exchange of conversation, news, arguments, and gossip. How different from today's mechanized ringing up of sanitized parcels carried on a conveyor belt. Wooden carts are a simpler design architecturally than, say, the A&P, but their very simplicity is what allowed for a diversity in levels of exchange and communication.

High in the attic apex of the Methodist Church is an unmistakable nineteenth-century signature, scrawled in chalk across a massive hand-hewn rafter: "Thomas J. Coffin, 1830." The distinctive handwriting sends a chill up the spine and conjures up impressions of quill and ink, wooden barges, sails, riggings, shouts, hammers clanging, and honest sweat. Interwoven with that present experience

The vegetable carts on Main Street continue the market tradition of an earlier time.

is the universal past of a nation, the eternal presence of early America.

Nantucket was built at a time when people walked, and the streets developed in response to that pace and rhythm. The degree of interest and variety is geared for the speed of walking and lingering, and we might miss far too much detail when moving at a faster pace. The paths and ways that beckon to each traveler on the island are never singular but many. That is the real beauty of a journey of discovery on Nantucket: we are free to pick the routes we like the best. Some we choose for their directness, others for their shape or for shelter from the elements, and still others simply because we feel a special anticipation, a stirring in the heart and a pulling of the senses that compels us to move in that direction. In this way we can always find new and different intineraries to reach the same destinations.

Mechanized activity seems inappropriate for the old town, for it is a contradiction in time. Just as we are transported quietly back into the eighteenth century, we see an automobile, and it instantly breaks the trance. The streets call for strolling and lingering. At many points the paths offer a variety of visual experiences: views through trees, through houses, fences, views in from the water, views out over the water, over the town. Some views are panoramic, while others frame a special event. In some the spectator plays a part. There are excellent panoramas from the hilltops. These are the points from which the island shows its true proportions, the merging of land and water, town and nature, and the cultural concept present in every

In the Neighborhoods

detail. The streets and lanes are seldom straight, and there is always something to catch our eye at the end. They are sometimes rhythmic with structures that are exactly the same in form. On many occasions the houses vary in line and form, creating for us a range of nooks and small open spaces stitched together by white picket fences. Long, straight roads have very little interest for us because in one glance the whole is understood; rather, we seek contrast, change, and the mixing of elements in the environment.

Some of the most memorable perspectives are those which set up tensions between the known and the unknown; for instance, roads that disappear behind trees or curve to reveal only a glimpse of detail. Among others, the following streets provide this experience:

Academy Lane	South Mill Street
Ray's Court	Step Beach
Flora Street	North Mill Street
Union, near Main Street	Gull Island Lane

We delight in surprises. They entice us to explore, to visualize and to fill the environment with our own meanings. We need to feel free to meander back and forth, either physically or in our imagination, not taking in everything with a single glance. The most delightful environments provide a difference in experience between where our feet are walking and what our eyes—and minds—are seeing. This is called mystery.

Nantucket Town is a complex play, at once a drama and a comedy, where nature, architecture, and people compose the three acts. Unlike a conventional play, however, the acts of Nantucket's drama are interwoven and simultaneous. It is difficult to behave ourselves in the audience and watch patiently, for it is only on the streets and lanes that we are allowed to discover the relationships among the players.

The following journeys are not meant to be definitive. On Nantucket the traveler should feel free to move and explore easily in time and space, and for this reason the journeys remain only descriptions and reflections. They are not detailed guided tours; rather, they identify neighborhoods and conversations in the environment, suggest possible explanations for their presence here, and point out the ordinary and often overlooked.

 Main Street Square

Perhaps the best place to begin a Nantucket journey is at Main Street Square. We might very well call this important node the nerve

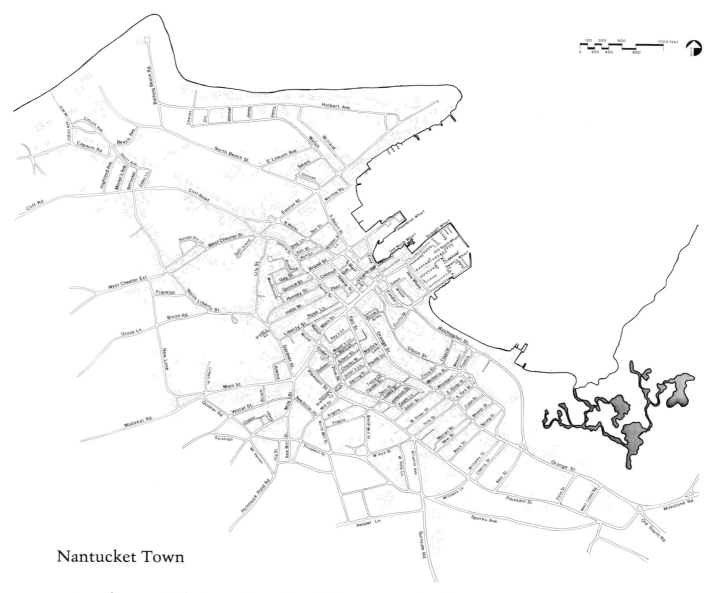

Nantucket Town

center of town. Today's activity, though intense, can hardly compete with the energy of days gone by. One glance 'round the square a hundred and fifty years ago would have taken in the shopkeepers scurrying out to meet the packets unloading vegetables and wares at the wharves; the town crier barking out the latest news and gossip from the continent; and the princely mansions, with their beckoning porticoes, lining the upper end of the street. Above the usual hum of commerce at this busy spot, we'd hear the bell of South Tower announcing noon, and the shouts, screams, and whoops arising when another whaling ship returns with its precious "greasy" cargo. Sounds must have been different then: click-clacking of horses's hooves and thump-thump of wooden wagon wheels over the cobbles.

In the Neighborhoods

79

Main Street Square.

We could have known who was coming just by the sound of his approach. Today's rubber tires mask these telltale sounds; after all, a Ferrari sounds the same as a Ford as it rolls slowly over the cobbles.

Once canopies extended out from the shops into the square's space, acting like welcoming arms. Goods were brought out onto the street, inviting active participation from passers by. Shoppers could browse at leisure among Indian spices, exotic fruits and vegetables, Chinese vases, and Italian silks as the square was enveloped in the homely smell of freshly baked bread. Just as in Old World cities today, chairs and tables were brought out into the public area. In a perceptual sense, this narrowed the space so that the observer could visualize both sides of the street at once. This is an important concern on shopping streets. Markets, parades, and ceremonies all found their home on Main Street. In a sense, the old square has been robbed of its original function and distinction by automobiles, which help to diminish this once important pedestrian domain.

The square's cobbles came to Nantucket as ship's ballast from Gloucester, and were laid in 1837. Following the Great Fire, the north side of the street was straightened and pushed back. The structures were rebuilt in the brick Greek Revival style we see today. This side of the square presents a uniform rhythm of bricks, facades, and gables, while the south side, built mostly after 1925, shouts a colorful

dialogue of diversity: pitched roofs alternate with flat roofs, and bricks contrast with clapboards, all taking place beneath the sentinel of Old South Tower. The broad sidewalks provide ample space for the furniture of this outdoor "room," and one thing has certainly not changed since the halcyon days of yore: we can still "sit and watch the pass." The parade we watch today is no less telling of our culture than were the fashions, costumes, and personalities of a century ago.

Almost medieval in its long narrow space, Main Street Square is capped at the ends by two important structures. At the east end is the Pacific Club, called the "Rotch Warehouse," and built around 1772. William Rotch, a whaling merchant and prominent Quaker, owned the ships *Dartmouth* and *Beaver*. In 1773, after delivering a cargo of whale oil to London, these same vessels, along with another ship, the *Eleanor*, were chartered by the East India Company to transport British tea to the American Colonies. This was not just *any* tea or *any* old ships, for their coincidence in Boston Harbor hosted the now legendary Boston Tea Party. From this modest building the ship *Bedford* was dispatched in 1782. It was the first to sail up the Thames hoisting the stars and stripes of the new American nation. The warehouse has had numerous functions and has changed owners several times over the last two hundred years. Perhaps it serves best, though, as a fitting anchor for the old market square.

The Pacific Bank, built in 1818, sits at the opposite end of the square. The institution's name came about because so much Nantucket money was earned in the Pacific Ocean. With its curved Federal portico the Pacific Bank invites us to sit awhile on its steps

---

or to come inside. Both of these buildings function as gateways. The bank building marks the transition from the square to the expanse of Main Street and the remainder of town; the Pacific Club opens the door to the Harbor area.

All of the neighborhoods and districts in Nantucket are spun off in layers from this central square. A variety of functions and architectural styles swaddle the open space like elaborate packaging. Most all of the principal streets originate in this center, and they form a snakelike labyrinth that weaves through and defines the surrounding layers. The Harbor area lies to the east, the rebuilt center of town to the north, and the residential neighborhoods to the south and west.

The Harbor

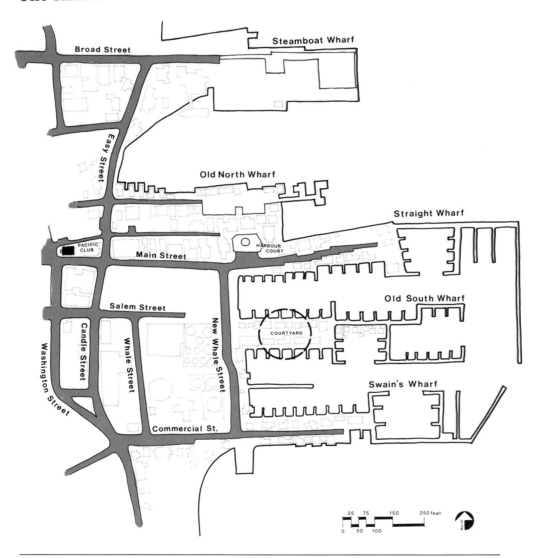

Nantucket's harbor presents an ever-changing image of lines, sheets, flags, and masts.

 The Harbor Area

The intersection of Main Street with New Whale Street presents us with a panorama of water and architecture, the merging of land and sea. To one side is Old South Wharf, and to the other lie Main Street and the gateway to Straight Wharf. If the old Main Street Square was the nerve center of town, the Harbor was certainly its heart and soul. This neighborhood is composed of five wharves, all rebuilt after the Great Fire. Here we can see numerous "conversations" taking place between architecture and water, interpreted for us through wharves, balconies, docks, and stairways.

It was once the place of incredible industry: the clanging of hammers, the furling of sails, the continuous knocking or rubbing of large wooden vessels on the docks filled the ears, and the persistent odor from the boiling try-pots invaded every pore. During the summer

A quiet moment in the courtyard at Old South Wharf.

months this neighborhood is still an area of intense activity, though now of a distinctly recreational nature. The monumental white yachts lining the wharves contrast in scale with the smaller, more colorful fishing vessels. They cause us to stop and wonder at the elegance of a contemporary life at sea. The Harbor, relatively dormant in the winter and fall with only a few fishing and lobster boats, becomes a unique integrated community during the summer months.

Old South Wharf is one of the most charming places to be in the summertime. Its composition is formed by a central courtyard with studios clustered around it. The little cottages are asymmetrically arranged—when one building pushes forward, another recedes, creating a pleasant, irregular facade for the central open space. Dappled sunlight falls through the trees, ocean breezes push past the cottages, and summer landscape textures grow up and over the architectural surfaces, enveloping them in a web of wild roses. The artists have made it their home by bringing their work out into the courtyard space. They blur the edge with lawn chairs and easels, just as natural textures soften the street edges in town.

Here we experience layers of views: a view over to Swain's Wharf, a glimpse back at South Tower, back at South Wharf. An entire community, a continuation of the town, has been brought out above the water onto piers. Each wharf can be seen as a street of sorts. The ships and boats in endless rows are like parked cars. Wharf buildings are human-scaled, and certainly more cordial to boats than they are to automobiles. Cars seem grossly out of place here; the architecture does not yield as easily to them as it does to the vessels.

The buildings in town stop directly on the street's edge. Not so at the Harbor, where the architectural edges reach out—to the water, over the water, to the boats—like plants turning to the sun for life. It is a different concept and a different rhythm.

A view of Straight Wharf from South Wharf.

     Straight Wharf contrasts sharply with Old South Wharf. It is actually an extroverted extension of Main Street over the water. As we pass through the gate, the floor texture changes, signaling that we have entered another territory. It is a streetscape, long and linear, with interchanging glimpses of cottage and sea. The seemingly indefinite edges converge on a broad wooden dock that extends far out into the water. Here we can experience the ever-present nautical textures: chains, riggings, ropes, nets, alternating with gulls and the occasional day's catch. The endless rhythm of blue-capped pylons leads us out to the very edge of man and sea.

     From the end of Straight Wharf we can see a spectacular panorama of the town. We are able to identify the Quanaty Bank, the changes in topography, and the layers of town. South Tower marks the center, as North Tower distinguishes Beacon Hill. A brief glance from this vantage point immediately establishes the order and character of the old town. Looking out to sea, we can make out the house edges of Monomoy to the south, the scalloped finger of Coatue

straight ahead, then move our gaze slowly over the expanse of water to rest on Brant Point and the miniature white lighthouse. Turning to look back on the town will reveal a Gordian knot of wharves, lines, hulls, pylons, shingles, and foliage, with both North and South towers rising above the rest of the composition. As we return to town, South Tower remains the landmark constantly in view, guiding us back.

In the moments just before sunset, the buildings on Old North Wharf take on a special glow.

Easy Street projects a completely different feeling. After passing briefly through townscape, the street opens to reveal yet another seascape, completely different in character and form from the others. It is appropriate that there are benches here, for this is one of the most serene spots in town. Here a friendly collision of architectural forms challenges the water with balconies and boat launches. Light quality, too, is different, as the scene never receives direct sunlight. Dancing reflections on the water are enhanced by the shadows and northern light. The buildings and sea actually change color and character with different light—morning, evening, storm, bright sun, sunset. White trim outlining the buildings seems very bold; it must be, or the light reflections would negate the buildings' depth and the expanse of grey would merge into one giant mass. This is a sheltered harbor, secure in its surroundings of buildings to each side, but expansive in the water's endless horizon. For many people this

The Nantucket Experience

panorama is a personal landmark, a place to watch the sun come up, the colors change silently throughout the day, and to sit and contemplate beginnings and meanings with their backs resting easily against the hustle and bustle in the center of town.

⬟ Town Center

After the passing of the whaling era, activity on Nantucket shifted inland to the center of town. The once international port has now become an international visitor's center where we are just as likely to meet someone from the Netherlands or Japan as from Nebraska. The neighborhood bordered by the Harbor, Broad Street, Centre Street, and Main Street comprises the heart of what was destroyed by the Great Fire of 1846. The Nantucketers wasted no time and spared no money in rebuilding this neighborhood, and its function, its scale, its architecture, and its character are completely different from the

Town Center

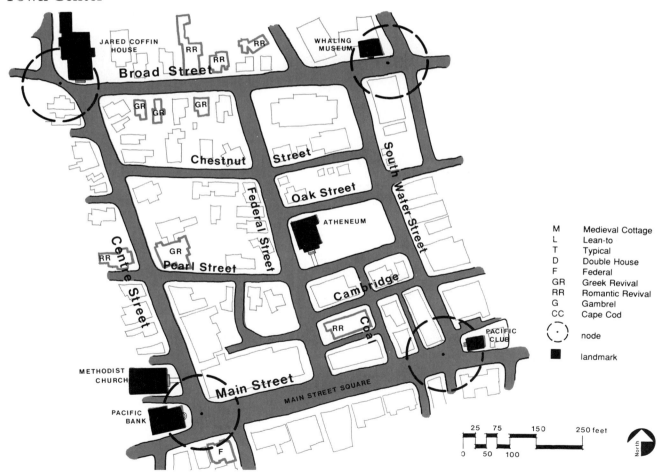

M	Medieval Cottage
L	Lean-to
T	Typical
D	Double House
F	Federal
GR	Greek Revival
RR	Romantic Revival
G	Gambrel
CC	Cape Cod
⟨·⟩	node
■	landmark

areas that surround it. In a sense, the small center is really a kind of landlocked commercial island, and it has an intriguing split personality. The once-important candle factories, warehouses, cooper shops, and shipping offices are now gift shops, ice cream parlors, bicycle rentals, and T-shirt shops. These sit side-by-side with a second group of buildings that includes the fish market, the post office, the library, and the corner drug store. When the first group closes for the long winter months, the second group blossoms forth, reasserting their importance, only to step down again on Memorial Day when the season officially begins and their neighbors open and shine once again. This cycle, like a sibling rivalry, has continued and intensified year after year.

For most people arriving by steamship, Broad Street provides the first indication of town. Walking off Steamboat Wharf, the traveler is greeted by the Peter Foulger Museum and the Whaling Museum. These stand as a gateway into town. Inside of the simple brick buildings can be found not only a compelling chronology of the town and

LEFT: Broad Street's Victorians invite the visitor to sit a while and contemplate the carefree activity along the street. RIGHT: The Jared Coffin House.

The Nantucket Experience

island, but several special elements that mark the high points of the community's history.

Broad street was widened after the fire, and its width makes it somewhat difficult for the buildings to "converse" across the street. However, with the shop windows and the colorful quarterboards that call out the shop names, the street does seem festive. Broad Street's buildings might resemble a group of adults at a party. The Greek Revivals are aligned along the south side, their dress serious and formal when compared to the explosion of ornament displayed on the two Victorians across the street. And although the older structures sport bright new paint, only the Victorians wear the party hats.

The Jared Coffin House stands solidly at the intersection of Broad and Centre Street. It was built in 1842 by Jared Coffin, then one of the wealthiest men on the island. Only ten years earlier, Jared had built the brick mansion "Moor's End" on Pleasant Street for his wife. Mrs. Coffin was accustomed to Boston Society and was never really happy there because she felt that Moor's End was too far from the activity in the center of town. Jared then built this house for her. Rumor had it that she didn't like it much better than the first, and in less than two years the Coffins moved back to Boston. A steamship company bought the structure and transformed it into a hotel. For nearly one hundred years it was called the "Ocean House," and catered to such dignitaries as Daniel Webster, Herman Melville, and Ulysses S. Grant. The Jared Coffin House is the only brick structure in this part of town. Its materials and imposing stature cause it to stand out, distinguished from the rest, a wayfinder in the neighborhood.

Federal Street long ago marked the water's edge and represented the shoreline of the Great Harbor. In 1743 the dunes were leveled for the creation of the Bocochico lots. After the 1846 fire, the street was widened, and this new width helps to bring the monumental scale of the Atheneum into proportion. The Great Fire had also destroyed the first Atheneum, but it was quickly rebuilt in this newer Classical style. "Our Lady of the Isle," the tiny Catholic Church, is a product of the Romantic era, a revival of Early Christian or Romanesque forms, translated in a very Nantucket way. Its texture and lines cause it to appear heavier and more stable than the white lofty Atheneum down the street. The lines of the church lead our eye down, visually anchoring the structure into the ground. By contrast, every line on the Classical structure leads our eye up to focus on the splendid temple front.

The cascading tree branches form a tunnel over the street in the summertime, and the sidewalk on the west side looks as if we are burrowing through foliage that separates architecture and street. Repeating rhythms of porches and fences remain intact almost to

"Our Lady of the Isle" is a neo-Romanesque structure translated in a very Nantucket way.

"Our Lady of the Isle" seems rooted to the ground, while the pristine cornice of its Greek Revival neighbor, the Atheneum, appears to soar upward.

Broad Street. Several little lanes run east and west from Federal Street. Some, true to the center's split personality, sleep during the cold months and remain only back alleys, but others such as Pearl and Chestnut streets, have distinctive charms all their own and refuse to give life up during the winter.

In July, Federal Street, like most of the town center, is filled with people wearing shorts and T-shirts, sometimes barefoot, carrying ice cream cones, sandwiches, and beach towels, or riding bicycles over the cobbles. December, on the other hand, presents us with different faces: babies bundled snug in carriages reach out to pet dogs on leashes; burly fishermen still in their hip-waders and red suspenders rush home, carting baskets of scallops; construction workers, librarians, accountants in tweeds, all greet one another as long-lost friends who haven't chanced to meet since Memorial Day.

A Stroll Down Main Street

Originally called State Street, this vital linear node is lined with magnificent old houses. It used to be the principal highway to the Great Harbor and was the hinge that linked the north and south parts of town. In many ways, it can be seen today as a "Hall of Stars" for Nantucket architecture. Balustrades, cupolas, roofwalks, porticoes, and stoops reach out, extending the Classic-inspired homes into our space. The architectural details alternate rhythmically with the splendid old elm trees.

The white Classical structure at 72 Main Street was built for John Wendell Barrett in 1820. Its double Ionic portico sets the scale

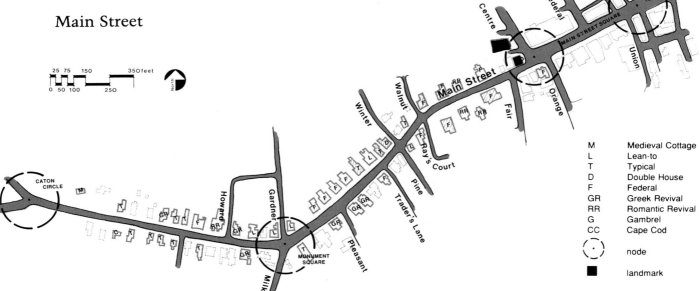

Main Street

M Medieval Cottage
L Lean-to
T Typical
D Double House
F Federal
GR Greek Revival
RR Romantic Revival
G Gambrel
CC Cape Cod

node

landmark

and character for the rest of the street. The mansion sits across from the Barney House, a Victorian-era structure. One can almost hear them conversing across the street, discussing the generation gap and quietly agreeing that there really isn't one, at least not here.

To be noticed on this avenue, a house had to be grand, or it would pale in comparison with its neighbors. The stature and dignity of even the very oldest homes have been carefully preserved. Judging by the elegance of these structures, we would never guess that most of their builders were not bankers, doctors, or barristers, but simple whaling men who made their living by sweat and manual labor. Some of the more restrained homes were built by Quaker merchants, the more elaborate by the World's People.

An engaging dialogue can be sensed between the two brick structures at 75 and 78 Main. The pair were built by Charles and Henry Coffin, two brothers. Though both houses were built around 1832 and are of a transitional Federal/Classical style, they reflect

The Nantucket Experience

subtle differences in the brothers' philosophies. The basic lines are nearly the same, but Charles was a Quaker and the details on his house remained simpler. He used only brownstone to frame the Classic doorway and windows, and he insisted on using a traditional roof walk. Henry, on the other hand, was long disassociated from the Society, and chose to display a Classical balustrade, cupola, and trim, and an elaborate marble entryway. Charles's house, the more humble one, sits back from the street, while Henry's appears more insistent, perched directly on the sidewalk's edge: two brothers, two houses, two philosophies.

Near the end of the street we are confronted by another architectural event. In 1836 Joseph Starbuck had three identical mansions built for his sons William, Matthew, and George, at numbers 93, 95, and 97. Tradition tells us that the elder Starbuck wanted his sons to remain in the family's business of whaling, and insisted that each one become a master cooper. Only when they had perfected their trade would he let them have their new homes. Though Classically inspired, the houses are of the Federal style. They sit directly on the sidewalk's edge, which reinforces their presence. On Nantucket they are fondly referred to as "the Three Bricks."

Directly across from these are two magnificent Greek Revival mansions. One of Joseph Starbuck's daughters married a man from Newport named William Hadwen. He built the house at number 96 for himself and his wife. The one next door, at number 94, was built later for their adopted daughter. Though these structures look very much alike, with their monumental temple fronts, they really have subtle

In the Neighborhoods

Looking across toward the Three Bricks from the porch of the Hadwen House.

"West Brick" in summer.

differences. Mr. Hadwen's mansion is wider and of the Greek Ionic order, and his daughter's house, though equally impressive, is of the Corinthian order.

LEFT: 105 Main Street, a Nantucket collage. RIGHT: Standing at 99 Main Street, looking east.

The relationship between the Two Greeks and the Three Bricks is like that of brothers and sisters. The brick houses are more masculine in appearance. They push forward and insist on being heard. The Greek Revivals appear slightly more feminine. They seem to defer to the trio of brick structures, as they are set back from the edge of the street, but their monumental scale guarantees them a powerful sense of presence.

The Civil War Memorial stands in the middle of Main Street and acts as a form of gateway marking the junction of many streets. We will pass into another area now, signaled by the different street surface. Nantucket was hailed a "banner town" of the Commonwealth for sending 339 men into the Union Army and Navy—fifty-six more than her quota. The monument, built in 1874, stands in memory of the seventy-four townsmen who gave up their lives in battle during the American Civil War. Its broad granite base is the millstone from the old Round-Top Mill that once stood on the site of the New North Cemetery. At one time the town hall (town "house," on Nantucket) stood opposite this monument, and the little square acted as a forecourt for the building.

Nantucket's Main Street presents an elegance and harmony of architecture and landscape unrivaled in many American towns. All at once it is a time machine, and if we squint our eyes, these very porticoes might conceal a young Quaker girl blushing at the sound of piano music, yet curious, with a faraway look in her eye; a sailor with money to spend, just returned from 'round Cape Horn and a four-year greasy voyage; a Starbuck family, somber and gray, walking to meeting, though the youngest son, Zebediah, would rather play marbles and stops frequently to pick up bugs; an aproned shop-keeper smiling as he leans in a doorway, because, after all, 1840 has been a very good year.

 Vestal Street

This country lane, much more informal than Main Street, is marked at the beginning by the Hinchman House, the Natural History Museum. The structure curves with the pavement edge, inviting us onto Vestal Street, where the rhythm is slower and the houses are spaced further apart. Number 1, a Typical Nantucket house, was once the home of Maria Mitchell. Born a Quaker and modest at heart, she was destined to become one of the most influential astronomers and educators of the mid-nineteenth century. So intent was she on learning that by fourteen years of age she was completely at home with astronomical calculations and navigational devices.

Maria was rarely idle. We can imagine her sitting in the tiny office adjacent to the front door, hunched over a desk piled high with calculations; darting to the roof of the Pacific Bank building where she peers through a telescope, sweeping the the clear skies over Nantucket; trudging back down Vestal Street, her cloak pulled tight against the wind, totally absorbed in a new and inspiring concept.

During one of her nocturnal watches on the roof of the bank building in 1849, Maria discovered a comet, and afterward her life was never quite the same. For her discovery, she was decorated by the King of Denmark and was also elected to the American Academy of Arts and Sciences, the first woman to have that honor. Later she was asked to accept a professorship at the newly formed Vassar College for women.

The very idea of educating women in the third quarter of the nineteenth century was controversial. Maria is thought to be the first woman college professor in America, though she was basically self-

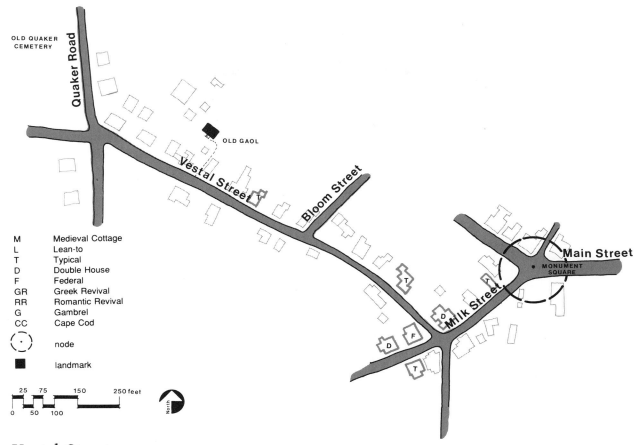

OLD QUAKER CEMETERY

Quaker Road

OLD GAOL

Vestal Street

Bloom Street

Milk Street

Main Street

MONUMENT SQUARE

M   Medieval Cottage
L   Lean-to
T   Typical
D   Double House
F   Federal
GR   Greek Revival
RR   Romantic Revival
G   Gambrel
CC   Cape Cod

(·)   node

■   landmark

25   75   150   250 feet
0   50   100

North

Vestal Street

educated. Despite the fact that she had been long disassociated from the Society for her worldly ways, Maria could not easily dismiss their basic beliefs of equality and education for all. She persisted in education reform. In short, she expected no less from her women students than she would from any man. To many of her students during the last century, this modest house remained a special shrine. It is fitting that it still stands as a lasting monument to one of America's brightest scholars.

The defined edges of Vestal Street begin to break down as the street curves and the houses push back from the edge on the south side. The first name for this street, Prison Lane, was more sober and certainly less tranquil than the present one. Both the old name and the presence of the jail project images of stripe-shirted convicts being led down the road in chains to work in the fields; however, historical accounts contradict this image, for the Quakers did not believe in cruel or inhuman punishment. The inmates were even allowed to go home at night in the winter and report back in the morning for incarceration. After all, there wasn't much chance for escape from the

In the Neighborhoods

island, as swimming was out of the question.

A wooden sign marks the entrance to the Old Gaol, and a narrow sand path leads to the building. We are confronted by a structure that looks similar to the ones surrounding it, but look closer: its walls are built of two layers of squared logs notched together at the corners, enclosing four tiny cells. Rusted iron straps brace the interior, and iron grilles bar the small windows. By its solid austerity, it must have made potential malefactors think twice before committing a crime on Nantucket.

The end of the lane intersects with Quaker Road, defining the edge of town and country. The panorama presents a sweeping view over the rolling moors to the west. Here is the Old Quaker Cemetery, guarded now only by an aging split-rail fence. The graveyard is silent, though so many stories ache to be told. There once was a young widow who, against the teachings of the sect, sneaked out one night and planted a wild rose bush on her husband's grave. She simply could not bear the thought of losing him forever. So strict was the ruling against grave markers that when the overseers discovered it they disassociated her immediately. Only a few humble stones appear now, set after the Quaker restrictions had lessened. Simple human stories are buried here, but the silence is broken only by the whistling winds that play over the grass and wildflowers.

 Mill Hill and Environs

Long ago, when there were four mills in operation on the hills overlooking town, an intricate radius of narrow lanes fanned out from the area around Pleasant Street, each terminating at a windmill. Before the foliage in town had grown so lush, these mills could be seen easily from the harbor, and they became wayfinders that marked the hilltops.[6] It was rumored that once during the Revolutionary War, the mill keepers set the vanes of the mills to point out the location of a British frigate in the waters off Nantucket. In whaling days, people used to climb to the top of the mills to watch for incoming ships, and children were dispatched to run to the captain's home to tell his family that he was "just comin' 'round the Point."

Today Pleasant Street forms the gateway to Mill Hill. The Two Greeks stand guard at the entrance on Main Street, and the path curves south with the topography. A view down the street focuses on Moor's End, the first mansion built by Jared Coffin. From the vantage point just past Main, we are able to look behind the Two Greeks and see how the characteristic Nantucket "warts" appear even on the stately houses facing Main Street. Their proper public faces shine brightly on the principal street, while the informal, sometimes chaotic arrangements of everyday life are tucked behind.

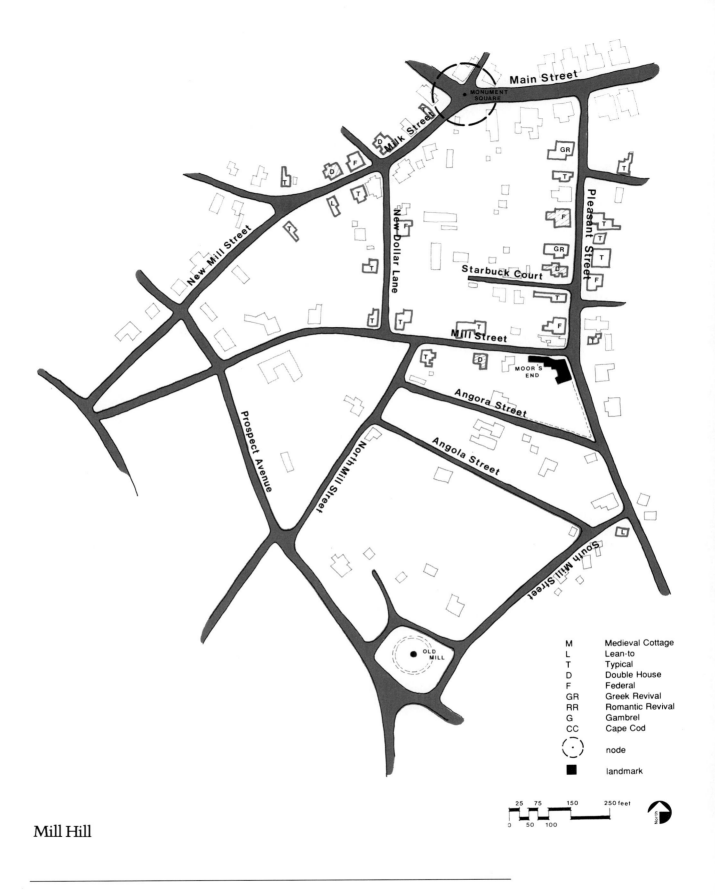

Main Street

MONUMENT SQUARE

Milk Street

New Mill Street

New Dollar Lane

Pleasant Street

GR

T

F

GR

G

Starbuck Court

T

Mill Street

F

T

D

MOOR'S END

Angora Street

Prospect Avenue

North Mill Street

Angola Street

South Mill Street

L

OLD MILL

M   Medieval Cottage
L   Lean-to
T   Typical
D   Double House
F   Federal
GR Greek Revival
RR Romantic Revival
G   Gambrel
CC Cape Cod

node

landmark

25   75   150   250 feet

0   50   100

North

Mill Hill

In the Neighborhoods

99

LEFT: The Isaac Macy House.
BELOW LEFT: Occasional Victorian details stand out on Pleasant Street, where most of the houses predate the Civil War.
BELOW RIGHT: A Typical Nantucket House on Mill Street.

The Nantucket Experience

At one time Pleasant Street formed the western edge of the West Monomoy lots. The houses on this street are larger than those on the surrounding area of Mill Hill, and are set directly on the sidewalk's edge. Isaac Macy built the impressive Classical house at number 7. Its portico and elegant proportions rival any found on Main Street.

Wálter Folger—a descendant of Peter Folger and cousin of Maria Mitchell—once lived across from the Macy house, in the Typical Nantucket at number 8. He was a brilliant man, at once a mathematician, surveyor, lawyer, philosopher, and talented inventor. On a visit to the island, Daniel Webster was so taken with the local genius that he wrote about Folger in his memoirs. A few of his inventions can still be found in the Peter Foulger Museum.[7] Perhaps it was from Walter that Maria received her inspiration and her love of science.

Houses from all generations and levels of prosperity line this street, where Quakers and World's People lived side-by-side. Starbuck Court, named for Joseph Starbuck, was once bordered by his warehouses, candle factories, and shops. This little lane originally ran through to New Dollar Lane.

Moor's End was so named because at the time of its construction it stood at the edge of the wilderness. This brick Federal house, peeking out from behind the trees, contrasts sharply in scale and materials with its immediate surroundings. The estate boasts the largest enclosed garden on the island, complete with garden house and carriage house. With its elaborate white cupola and balustrade, Moor's End stands out, and like the Jared Coffin House, it becomes a landmark in this neighborhood.

Following along the edge of Moor's End on Mill Street, we come upon what appears to be an old rural commons bordered by small houses. This was an important node in days gone by. From this spot radiated most of the lanes that led up to the windmills two centuries ago. The Typical Nantucket houses resting on the street edges reinforced the spider pattern of the streets. Today this space still provides a moment of tranquility and a quiet spot for reflection. Mill Street continues up and curves around the pasture, exposing only pitched roofs and chimneys. North Mill runs nearly perpendicular to Mill Street. A split-rail and a running board fence converge on a narrow, sandy path that winds and climbs the hill to disappear into a clump of trees. This path was called Brimstone Lane, and ran up the hill to the spot where the old Brimstone Mill used to be.

New Dollar Lane also fronts this pastoral scene. Two Typical Nantucket houses mark the gateway onto this street from Mill Street. The house that Job Macy built sits on the west corner. Job was the young Quaker who disregarded his father's advice and tradition

by building his house with two stories front and back. The structure looks so unimposing and modest by today's standards that we're perplexed at how it could offend even the Quakers' rigid code of behavior.

Rural in detail, New Dollar Lane was formerly called Risdale Street. Almost all of the residences in this area were also shops at one time. The coopers, blacksmiths, boatwrights, and housewrights all worked here; it was not always the sleepy neighborhood that it appears today. The white clapboarded Federal style house that dominates the middle of the block belonged to Joseph Starbuck, builder of the Three Bricks on Main Street. From this rather modest structure, Joseph held a firm reign on the family business. Its simple lines, though modified over the years, contrast with the more refined ones of the Three Bricks. Perhaps the Main Street houses reflect Joseph's later wealth. Most of the activity here during the last century centered on whaling in some way, and the tight edges of the street are appropriately formed by a ship's rail fence.

South Mill Street probably dates back to the construction of the mill in 1746. The street rises up to the landmark, and the houses are

set at an angle, welcoming us into its domain. Swain's Mill remains the constant focal point. We catch glimpses of it behind the houses, a solitary figure against the changing palette of the sky. Sunsets silhouette its form, providing a stark vision of its utility but nothing of its character or texture.

The mill's silhouette offers an interesting reminder. The Quakers abhorred art of any kind, yet, oddly enough, they allowed silhouettes. Perhaps this was because, like the sunset image of the

In the Neighborhoods

mill, a silhouette defines only the edge. The vision is impersonal, and though accurate in outline, it cannot possibly reveal any beauty or detail.

The climax of a journey down South Mill Street comes when we climb to the top of the mill and look out over the rooftops of most of Nantucket Town. From here our gaze encompasses all the enveloping layers of town. In winter we are presented with a collage of pitched roofs outlined in white and spiked by brick chimneys. The summer foliage, conversely, captures most of the image like dense green clouds, allowing only momentary hints of architecture to peek through the top.

Believed to have been built of timbers from wrecked ships, Swain's Mill is the last remaining of Nantucket's five windmills. Here we can sit and watch the huge vanes turning in the wind and listen to the clack-clack of the intricate old wooden machinery, the rustling of the sails, and the sound of stone grinding stone. We can visualize what a day's work might have been like before the advent of factory production, before mass-marketing strategies and chain-store economics. And sitting amongst the grass and wild flowers, clicking off each turn of the vanes, we might as well contemplate the ephemeral nature of progress.

◆ The Original Fishlots

The Fishlots subdivision, marked off in 1717, extended north and south between Ray's court and today's Eagle Lane, and east and west between Pine Street and the Quanaty Bank, later to Orange Street. A more casual atmosphere can be experienced in this tight residential neighborhood, where most of the houses date from the very early periods of the town's history. During the last century it was the most densely populated area in Nantucket. It was home to the tradesmen, the sailors, and the schoolteachers.

Each of the streets is unique and offers a different visual experience. Most have caps at the ends or focal points so that our eyes do not stray from the street edges. Orange, Fair, and Pine streets are the principal paths, and run from Main Street south to the edge of town. The smaller lanes join them like rungs in a curious bent ladder. It is on these miniature lanes that the true rhythm and essence of the neighborhood is felt. Their personalities can be almost rural and dense with foliage that completely works through the edges, as seen for instance on Ray's Court, Mott Lane, and Mooer's Lane. Martin's Lane has almost a northern European feeling with its small scale and brick street surface, and Hiller's Lane and Darling Street provide tiny versions of nineteenth-century city streets.

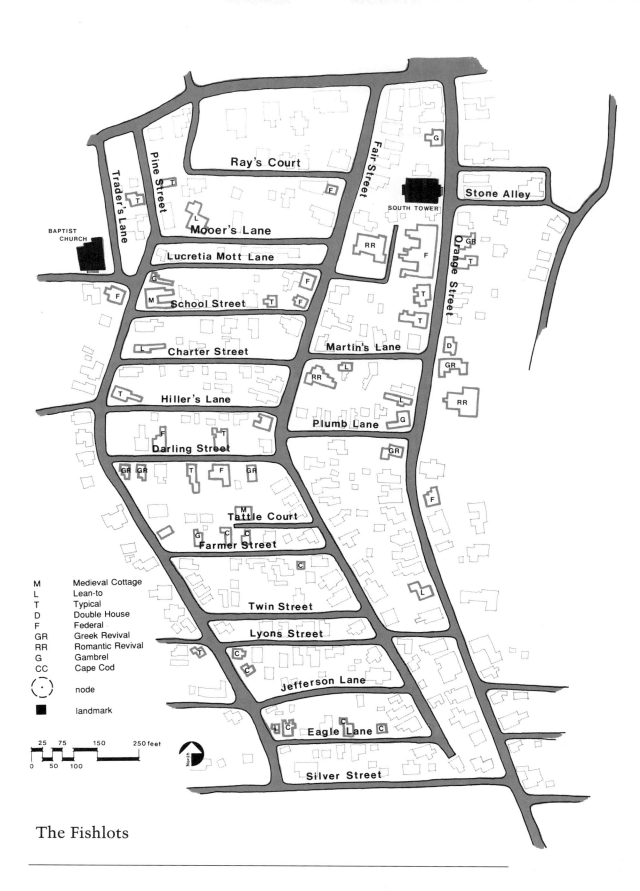

The Fishlots

The Fishlots neighborhood contains the majority of island churches. As the Quaker faith died out shortly after the turn of the nineteenth century, the Baptists, the Congregationalists, the Methodists, the Episcopalians, and the Catholics moved to the island and established followings. Here we can see an example of church architecture in the Federal, the Classical, and the Romantic Revival styles. The monumental scale of these three churches, moreover, creates an interesting contrast with the smaller Lean-tos and Typical Nantucket houses. Some of the structures were later embellished with Federal, Classical, or Victorian details, but the lines of these simple houses have remained nearly the same over the years.

Early in this century, a Nantucket woman named Harriet Barnes Thayer resided for a short time in England. Often she would stroll along the streets in Essex and Cambridgeshire, thinking about the little island far away. She marveled at how similar the English houses were to her very own Nantucket house. Once invited inside an Essex dwelling, she found her impression silently confirmed. Later, when Mrs. Thayer returned to Nantucket, she reminisced

The Nantucket Experience

about that English experience and recorded some of what she had been feeling at the time:

> You need not show me the way about this house. I know where all the rooms are, the little painted stairs, the white panelled rooms on either side the entry, the St. Domingo black mahogany table, the pink lustre cup and saucer on the mantel shelf, the white washed beams overhead. I could find my way blindfolded to the stand between the two front windows and lay my hand on the white coral shell piece under a glass shade. They would all be there, and often the blackened portrait over the fireplace.
>
> I do not need to be shown the face there. I know it. Grandfather or great grandfather, stout (in the old sense of the word implying some mental as well as physical quality), firm-lipped, with a good coat of tan, a shining glimpse of linen at the throat, a nose inclined to Roman, fearless, honest eyes, blue or brown, and with tell-tale lines at the corners that show in spite of the stiff upper lip, a devil of wit held down by a strong hand.[8]

When her British hostess had brought out some of the family heirlooms and treasures to share with her, Mrs. Thayer again mused to herself:

> . . . The sampler worked by a good girl, the model of a full-rigged ship, the Chinese ivory box, the silk shawl from Canton, the Indian bracelet, and I could hardly make my hostess believe that my own home, with the Atlantic between us, was nevertheless built just like hers. The corner cupboards held the same treasures, and my piece of white coral under a glass shade, was even larger than hers, and the portrait of Great-grandfather with a spy glass, was own brother to many such a one hanging over familiar mantel shelves thousands of miles away.[9]

As we stroll through these narrow Nantucket lanes, we, too, might imagine what it would have been like to meander through an English seaport village early in the nineteenth century: the children rushing off to school, books flying and dogs yapping at their feet; women shaking out rugs on their front stoops or exchanging letters, news, and information from the incoming packets; and artisans working their crafts—until the whole became enveloped in a symphony of hammers resonating with anvils, saws, planes, and the roar of bellows.

Orange Street is the principal path of the neighborhood. It was opened around 1723 with the West Monomoy Lot divisions, and runs south, curving with the bank. All of Nantucket's architectural styles can be seen along this street. The houses, characteristically resting on the sidewalk's edge, might represent a row of old sea captains. Each stern and upright public facade conceals smiles, tragedies, and adventures, for at one time more than a hundred captains had their homes on Orange Street. One can imagine that ghosts still gather to rock to and fro on the stoops and spin their yarns from 'round Cape Horn, Fiji, and the Japans.

Old South Tower, the dominant landmark of Nantucket, stands at the beginning of the street, seeming to gently protect the neighborhood and watch over the activity below. The main body of the church is of the Federal style and dates back to 1809. Unlike the other churches in town, which have forecourts, the Second Congregational Church sits on the street's edge, in line with the endless row of captains, and this placement increases its monumental presence. In 1812, a church committee purchased the Portuguese bell that rings out morning, noon, and curfew. An amusing story about this bell gives us an insight into the colorful character of the Nantucketers in the last century.

It seems that after the bell had arrived, the congregation needed to solicit funds to have a tower built and the bell installed. Its sound was particularly full and resonant, and the bell's arrival and delayed installation became known in Boston, where a prosperous congregation had just built a new church. The building committee in Boston wrote to the Nantucket congregation saying that they had a fine new church, and asked if the Nantucket society wanted to sell its bell. The Nantucketers sent their reply out directly on the next packet. Imagine the look on the faces in Boston when the Nantucketers' curt reply was read aloud: "We have a fine old bell, would the Boston society like to sell their church?" Pride aside, it took the congregation three years to install the bell; then in 1830, the tower had to be rebuilt to sustain its weight.

A curious concrete building with a little temple front stands near the beginning of Fair Street, at the intersection of Ray's Court. This structure looks out of place until we realize that it was built to house what was left of the historical holdings from the original Atheneum. The Fair Street Museum was built long after the Great Fire, of concrete to be fireproof. The old wooden Quaker Meeting house stands in front of the museum, and contrasts with the newer structure. In its stark simplicity it is a telling reminder of that austere way of life. We can imagine the men and women silently lining those stark benches, each waiting for a sign from God to speak at meeting. Sometimes entire meetings would pass with no one feeling compelled to speak; preparatory thoughts and lectures were seriously forbidden.

A stone marker was set in front of the structure in 1840 by William Mitchell, father of Maria. He placed both this small marker and the stone on Main Street, near the side of the Pacific Bank. These are called the Meridian Stones, and a line connecting them will indicate true north.

St. Paul's Episcopal Church, built in 1902, sits diagonally across the street from the meeting house. Their juxtaposition provides a lively dialogue between the two faiths. Like the tiny Catholic church in the town center, St. Paul's was designed in the Romanesque Revival manner. Unlike the Catholic Church, however, its granite construction is a more traditional application of this Romantic style. The prototype for this turn-of-the-century church survived in Europe from around 1000 to 1200 A.D. The heavy walls and turreted tower of St. Paul's are last vestiges of the days of battering rams and crossbow warfare. Moreover, the use of rough stones not only makes the building appear older than it really is, but certainly heavier and with a greater sense of purpose.

Two young people who would later become legends in American history lived on this street. In 1793, Lucretia (Coffin) Mott was born on Nantucket, and her birthplace once stood at the intersection of Fair Street and Mott Lane. The old Nantucket house was demolished years ago, but the principles and beliefs held dear by Lucretia have consequences down to our very day. Called by Emerson "the flower of Quakerism," Lucretia was instilled with a Nantucket sense of dignity and fair play. This young woman was to become one of the most outspoken abolitionists of the nineteenth century, often arguing at great odds for the basic equality of everyone regardless of color, race, creed, or sex. True to her Quaker upbringing, she worked long and hard for social reform. However, Lucretia is most notably remembered for her work with Elizabeth Cady Stanton and Susan B. Anthony in founding the Women's Suffrage Movement.

As a young man Rowland (Hussey) Macy lived along this street. He tried many occupations—whaling, gold mining, shopkeeping—all to no avail. After traveling to California and experiencing failure in his business, he left in 1858 for New York City. Rowland soon opened a small dry goods store in the lower east end. This tiny store blossomed into the impressive structure that stands today on the corner of Broadway and 34th Street. The name Macy's is now synonymous with department store, and that old island name is well-known from coast to coast.

Pine Street marked the western edge of the Fishlots subdivision. Near the opening of this street can be seen the third church, the Summer Street Baptist Church. Its frame was brought over from Maine in 1840. The structure was built with Classical influence, and in keeping with this tradition, the church is pristine white. A portico was part of the congregation's original plan, but the cost prohibited its actual construction. The once lofty spire was taken down during a strong gale years ago. Even so, the structure has never lost its original stature and dignity.

This street was a Coffin neighborhood. Through their houses we might understand how time and prosperity affected one Nantucket family. "Parliament House," the home of Mary and Nathanial Starbuck, rests at number 10 Pine. It originally stood near the head of Hummock Pond in Old Sherborne. After the town was relocated, this house was moved to Pine Street and enlarged. The basic Medieval Cottage can barely be seen through all the later embellishments. Town meetings, Quaker First Day meetings, and large family gatherings all took place in this noble old homestead before the turn of the eighteenth century. Mary Coffin Starbuck, called simply "the Great Mary," was Tristram's daughter and one of the island's first Quaker preachers. With her heritage and marriage, she combined the wealth and ingenuity of two famous island families.

Mary's grand-nephew, Benjamin Coffin, conducted classes on School Street. This wise old patriarch was the grandfather of Lucretia Mott. In 1756, Benjamin's son, Micajah, built the Lean-to house at number 14. An educated man, Micajah was a ship's captain, a statesman, a lawmaker, and the island's representative in Boston. He had

Doorways represent the transition between the outside world and the inside world, and therefore even the simplest doors present a ceremonious aspect.

many children, but of all his sons, Zenas emerged as the one most intrigued by the sea. The boy, raised in the Quaker faith, was destined to amass the largest fortune ever probated on Nantucket. In the early 1800s he built his house at number 9. True to the Quaker beliefs against worldly possessions and despite the builder's great wealth, the house was designed in a very modest Federal style. Though formal in its symmetry, the structure was sheathed in traditional shingles at a time when clapboarding was the more common treatment.

Zenas' sons, Charles and Henry, built the two Classic-inspired brick mansions on Main Street. One son continued the family Quaker tradition. His house, though impressive, shows a restraint of decoration. The younger son, ever so slightly, crept out from under the restrictions to produce a similar structure, though contemporary in every detail. Each generation in this Coffin family became a little more worldly and a little more prosperous; nevertheless, for the most part, they retained the Quaker conservatism. Their entire family history, as well as the history of architecture on Nantucket ,can be traced through the structures that they left behind.

All That Remains of the Original Wescoe Lots

The Wescoe Acre Lots were the first subdivision laid out in town. Running east and west between Federal and North Liberty streets, and north and south between Broad and Main streets, the thin lots were popular and quickly settled after the town had relocated to the Great Harbor. The parcels were very narrow, just two rods, or thirty-three feet, wide. All of the streets in this neighborhood have evolved from the seventeenth-century lot line divisions. They began as footpaths, separating one family's share from another; later they were used for cart traffic, and eventually the most popular ones became recognized as public streets and lanes.

The Great Fire destroyed all of the houses along Centre Street and a few of the structures to the west. Its line of destruction can easily be distinguished by the sharp contrast in architectural styles between the Greek Revival shops on Centre and the older Typical Nantucket houses on the adjacent streets running west. The rhythm seems to quicken along these streets because there is little foliage for our eyes to linger around. In addition, the houses are set mostly on the path's edge, and very few are turned to face south. Unlike the homes found in the Fishlots, the houses in this neighborhood, though basically the same forms and styles, are much larger. Their size might indicate a greater wealth or the owner's standing in the community.

Centre Street near Main was once called "Petticoat Row," because the majority of the shops were owned and run by women.

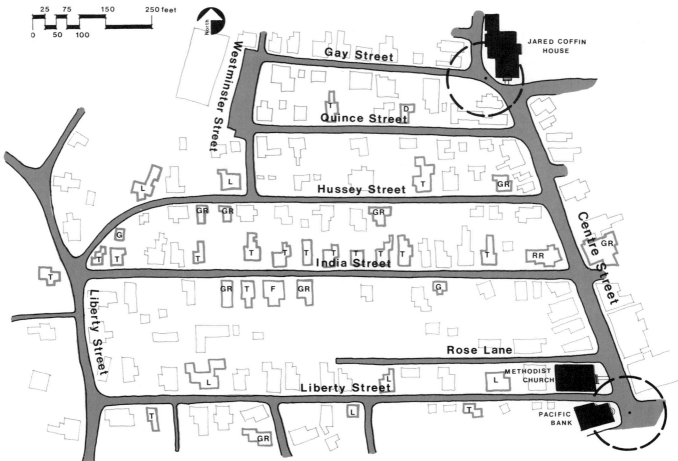

Wescoe Acres

As the men were often at sea for upward of three years, the women on Nantucket had greater responsibilities and played a larger role in town industries than on the mainland. This street, laid out with the subdivision in 1678, is one of the oldest thoroughfares in the community. All of the shops, however, are Greek Revivals and Victorian influenced, and most have their gables turned toward the street in the Classical Greek way. In town, Centre competes with Federal as a shopping street, and like Broad Street, it is indeed festive, with shop awnings in many different colors.

The Methodist Church, built between 1822 and 1823, barely escaped destruction in the Great Fire. Its grand Ionic portico was added in 1840, and because of this addition, the roofline was also changed. An inspection in the attic reveals that the carpenters simply built the massive new roof on top of the older hip-style roof. The original form and roof shingles are completely intact beneath the new one.[10]

M	Medieval Cottage
L	Lean-to
T	Typical
D	Double House
F	Federal
GR	Greek Revival
RR	Romantic Revival
G	Gambrel
CC	Cape Cod
(·)	node
■	landmark

The Classical portico looks as if it should be carved of stone; in fact, the columns' size and design were copied from stone pattern books shipped over from England. So precise is the carving that only the occasional peeling paint reveals the structure to be wood. The colossal columns give the Methodist Church a monumental scale, and like the Atheneum nearby, it looms larger than it really is. A good comparison can be made with the Pacific Bank, which was built in the

In the Neighborhoods

earlier Federal style. Its textured bricks and flat, overhanging roof bring the building down to our scale. It appears heavier, solid, as a bank should be. The white church, on the other hand, seems to soar from its very foundations, all eyes are directed up. Because the structure is set back from the street, its scale is not really overwhelming. In sympathy, the entabulature of the church was aligned with the edge of the roof on the bank. Even though the Church's colossal Ionic columns dwarf the tiny Ionic portico on the bank, the buildings communicate easily with one another. The bank presses forward, the church, up. Each gesture fits the building's intended function. They sit side-by-side like a couple married for years; the romance ebbed long ago, but the comfortable relationship will continue forever.

The Jared Coffin house marks a strong focal point at what appears to be the end of the street. In summer, the brick mansion pokes through and over the foliage, and the noon sun electrifies the facade until it shimmers and shines.

Diagonally across from the Jared Coffin House is the Seven Sea's Gift Shop, once the home of Captain George Pollard. The tragic story of his command of the whaleship *Essex* was immortalized by Herman Melville in his novel *Moby Dick*. Later, after having survived yet another shipwreck, Captain Pollard retired from the sea and became one of Nantucket's night watchmen. In his last years he could be seen roaming the blackened streets at midnight, his lantern held aloft to reveal a haunted face marked forever by nature's cruel fate.

The spire of North Tower comes into view from this point, and we think the street should appropriately end at the landmark hotel.

However, characteristic of Nantucket streets, it zigs and zags around the structure, and in so doing continues into another neighborhood that is functionally, stylistically, and rhythmically different from Centre Street in town.

The Pacific Bank and the Methodist Church have stood side-by-side for over 150 years.

The most curious route is experienced on Liberty Street, which runs due west, then angles sharply to the north, becomes North Liberty Street, weaves a little, then eventually stops at Cliff Road. This street once marked the southern and western edge of Wescoe Acres, and like Centre Street, it was laid out in 1678. The cobbles still remain intact for nearly one-third of the way. It is a telling experience to round the corner of Liberty Street and watch the grand portico of the Methodist Church merge into a wall of rough shingles. It lends a humanness to the otherwise monumental structure. Older homes line the north side of the street, and their parlors take full advantage of the sun's daily path. Newer houses in the Greek Revival and Victorian styles are found on the south side of the street.

India Street is perhaps the most memorable town street in Nantucket. Its name was Pearl Street until the mid-nineteenth century, when many island streets were renamed. Some were named after a particular family that lived on the street; others for a certain

In the Neighborhoods

Number 15 Liberty Street is one of the first Lean-tos converted into a double house on Nantucket, and remains splendid in every detail.

ship's captain; and still others, like India Street, for images and concepts that existed halfway around the world. Of a prosperous captain on Nantucket it might be said that "he is an East India Captain," indicating a rich and special breed. Joseph Sansom, a journalist for the Portfolio, once called Pearl Street "India Row," because the residents seemed to live in such ease and comfort. The name was wholeheartedly adopted. Mr. Sansom also wrote in 1811 that "Every house in this seafaring place had a look-out on the roof, or a vane at the gable end, to see when the ships have arrived from sea, or whether the wind was fair for the packets."

On India Street many of the old roof walks have been taken down. Nevertheless we can still imagine the scene long ago with handsome young captains atop these walks with long-glasses glued to their eyes, anxiously awaiting the day when they can finally return to sea. Women and children, bundled tight against the winds, pass up through the scuttles in the roofs and scan the waters for the barest trace of line or sail or the top of a mast, and often, in the end, express silent disappointment when day after day nothing is seen but the endless horizon.

Many of the houses on India Street are Typical Nantuckets and are predominantly four bays wide. Some of these homes were built and owned by Quakers, while others belonged to the World's People. Each house, though similar in line, is subtly different in detail from its neighbors. The more humble Typical Nantuckets at numbers 21, 23, 29, and 33, were Quaker influenced. Those with Classical embellishments such as porticoes, quoins, and clapboards were built

or later remodeled by non-Quakers. The continuous row of similar houses displays a lyrical rhythm of architecture, with the beat marked by stoops and porticoes. Window openings remain consistent, providing a complete melody for the movement and countermovement of the forms. Because all of the houses are nearly the same in height and picket fences hold the vertical edge where a house is set farther back, the street's rhythm is quickened and accentuated. The ancient Gambrel at number 18 becomes special, for it projects further into the streetscape and breaks the otherwise clean lines. In the same way, the house at number 27 seems bolder and heavier than its neighbors because of the quoins that emphasize its corners. India Street is really about rhythm and line. The pace is quick as all of the architectural edges converge upon a Typical Nantucket house at the end. A kind of one-point perspective is produced, and it sweeps our eye along the facades, causing the street to appear longer than it really is.

In the Neighborhoods

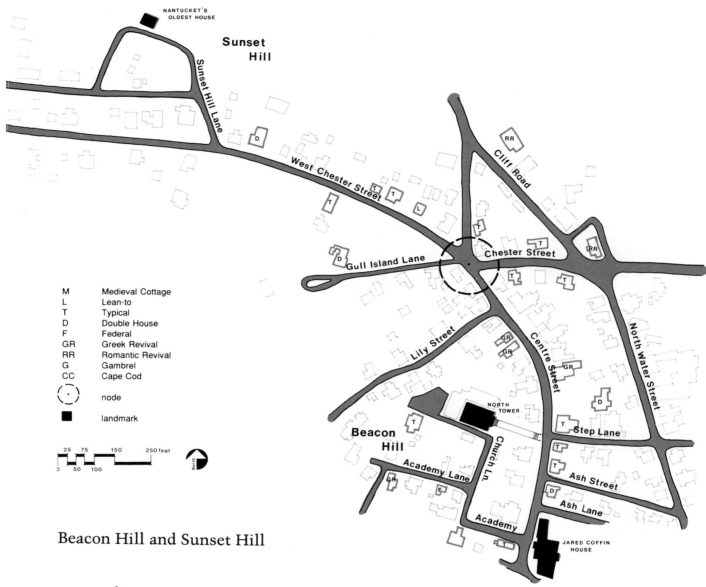

Beacon Hill and Sunset Hill

Beacon Hill and Sunset Hill

Centre Street weaves around the Jared Coffin House, seemingly to become another street. Instead, the name remains Centre, though we can easily tell that we have moved into a distinctly different part of Nantucket Town. During the Great Fire the Jared Coffin House served as a firebreak; therefore, most all of the structures behind it survived the blaze. Many were early Typical Nantucket houses that have been enlarged into double houses over the years.

Just past the intersection with Broad Street is Academy Lane, another of Nantucket's whimsical streets. Its course turns at an

abrupt angle, then turns again and continues. Through years of use, the cobbles have now settled into deep, uneven ruts. This path leads up to Church Lane and the First Congregational Church, which sits atop Beacon Hill. Behind the church, and set at an angle to it, is the Old North Vestry, built early in the eighteenth century. Adjacent to the ancient structure sits the Captain Reuben Bunker house. This

In the Neighborhoods

The Captain Reuben H. Bunker House, built c. 1820.

house was built just after the turn of the nineteenth century as a Typical Nantucket house. Less than twenty years later it was remodeled into a Federal style, complete with portico, elliptical fanlight, quoins, and clapboards. Though it is not actually symmetrical, its proportions are certainly elegant. The little house is a jewel, with its bright yellow paint, white trim, roof walk, and ship's-rail fence.

As has been mentioned above, we tend to think of buildings as having personalities: some are friendly, some are hostile, they can seem smug, intellectual, or just plain boring. How we determine a structure's character depends on how we perceive the building, and on the mood we are in at the time. Often when we look at the built environment we catch only momentary impressions of the structures. This means that buildings act, to a certain degree, like billboards that advertise what can be found inside of them. Unless we really want to explore further, one look is usually enough to tell us if we are going into the right building or not.

Just the quickest glance will tell us that the Old North Tower is a church. The single most important symbol of its function is the white steeple. But suppose we wanted to find out more about this church. If we looked at it in a photograph instead of in its setting, would we know that this structure was built on the East Coast or the West Coast? Hard to say. We intuit its context by associations. Already the mind considers the possibility that this church could be as old as 150 years. We eye the construction and settle on some time in the early 1800s. We then begin to wonder what denomination built it, Catholic or Protestant? We reason that Protestant churches tend to

The Nantucket Experience

The Old North Church, built in the early nineteenth century, stands as a landmark on Beacon Hill.

void of surface decoration save for the tracery windows; therefore, we surmise that it was built by a congregation adhering to Protestant ideals. After we figure out what it is and where it fits into the context of time, we begin to break down its composition into smaller pieces to record in our memory.

First of all, the structure is symmetrical and divided into three main sections, or a tripartite facade, with the entrance in the center section. This gives us an indication of how the interior might be arranged. Corresponding to what is revealed on the outside, the interior is one central hall with two narrower side aisles. When we put the pieces of the facade together, they become a rectangle standing on end in front of a triangle. On top of the rectangle is a cube, and a smaller cube is on top of the second one. Finally the whole composition is crowned by an elongated pyramid that forms a spire.

Now we might look even closer and discover that it is built of wood with a clapboard facade, and that the windows form pointed arches. The doorway, if looked at long enough, begins to resemble a person with arms open wide to receive visitors. We walk up the path and go inside. All of this takes place in the mind in less than a minute, but how often do we really take the time to analyze something in this detailed manner? Yet it is the way we understand architecture, or for that matter anything unknown, including people.

Perhaps the most dominant house on the street sits diagonally opposite the church at number 51 Centre. The house sits as far back from the street as does the church. Built for Peter Folger II around 1765, it is a three-and-a-half-story Typical Nantucket house. When the structure was first built, it was called the "flatroof" house, for it had only a form of balustrade or railing around the roofline. The present roof was added after the turn of the nineteenth century. Following the line of Centre Street, the remainder of the houses ride the edge as the street curves with the topography. By its placement, the house at 51 Centre creates a pause in the conversation of the houses, the rhythm stutters, then slowly picks up again.

At the midpoint of north Centre Street, we are greeted by an animated dialogue between twin Greek Revival houses. One is appropriately named "the Chatterbox." Absolutely identical in every detail, down to the ship's-rail fence, they cause us to stop and take a double look. The houses resemble identical twins all dressed up in sailor suits and standing arm-in-arm. The one on the south, called "Lantern House," seems taller because of its position on the hill; it appears to lean toward the smaller one in a protective and brotherly way.

Gull Island Lane is an old path that once led out to a small island in the middle of the Lily Pond. The ancient split-rail fence can hardly hold back the abundance of foliage to the north, where at least fifty shades of green press onto the little cobblestoned path. The rural detail indicates that we have moved out of town and are now passing into the country.

West Chester Street is the oldest thoroughfare in town. At one time it was the main highway that led from the first Sherborne east to the Great Harbor. Today's West Chester is a sleepy residential area, hardly indicative of its onetime importance. A row of Typical Nantucket houses set up high on basements lines the north side of the street.

Just off West Chester Street is Sunset Hill Lane. If we follow this route up Sunset Hill, gradually the foliage begins to part and the asphalt street breaks down into cobbles. Rounding the bend, we are confronted by Nantucket's Oldest House. The stark lines on this old Medieval Cottage Style structure take us back over three hundred years. The house remains in its original location, though its lines have changed considerably from the time of its construction.[11] As had been mentioned earlier, this house was built for Jethro and Mary Coffin as a wedding gift from their fathers. Mary was Captain John

Gardner's daughter and Jethro was Tristram Coffin's grandson. Their 1686 marriage occurred after the stormy "half-share men revolt," and was seen as a reconciliation between Nantucket's full-share men and the half-share men.

LEFT: *Gull Island Lane.* RIGHT: *Nantucket's Oldest House.*

Sunset Hill marked the eastern extremity of old Sherborne. Out of the mainstream of town, this old house has withstood Nantucket's changing fortunes, countless storms, even a fire or two.[12] After the turn of the twentieth century, though, it was badly in need of repair. A descendant of Tristram purchased the house, and Alfred Shurrocks renovated it in 1928. Every detail, from the batten door to the chimney, reveals that it was cut and shaped by hand. No one really knows why the upside-down horseshoe decorates the massive chimney. Some historians have speculated that it was a symbol of good luck; however, if it is, the luck is running out. Others have suggested that perhaps it symbolized the unification of two powerful island families. Actually the design resembles more a wishbone than a horseshoe. A symbol for a very young couple to make a wish on: an appropriate symbol for new beginnings. For Mary and Jethro Coffin,

In the Neighborhoods

this house represented the beginning of their married life; for the Nantucketers of 1686, it represented the beginning of a time of peace after some very turbulent years; and for us today, this house is one of the very few that remain from our beginnings as an American civilization.

⬠ The Point and Cliff Areas

These neighborhoods are distinguished from the rest by their unique locations and topography. Not really parts of the old town, the Point and Cliff areas are connected to the center by just a few streets.

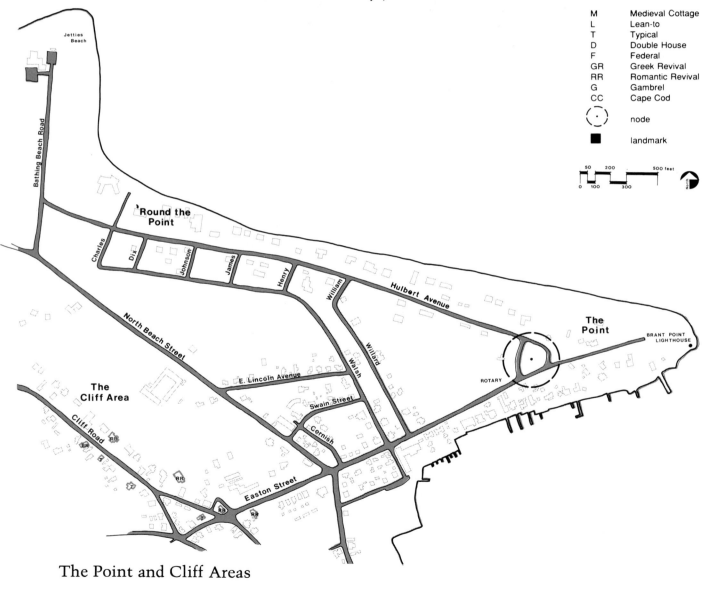

The Point and Cliff Areas

*Hulbert Street
houses reach out
to the north shore.*

Like the rest of town, these were places of great industry. Shipbuilding commenced on the Point in 1810. At the height of the whaling
industry, a ropewalk stood nearby and saltworks were located on
the harbor side. When the depression hit, however, the shops were
boarded up and forgotten until after the turn of the twentieth century.
When the summer people arrived, they experienced the area's wonderful views and ocean breezes and decided to build their vacation
homes here. One by one the houses sprang up along Easton Street,
and their styles are indicative of the times: Queen Anne, Shingle Style,
and a later form of East Coast Bungalow. Many are set back from the
street and have verandas or porches in place of the smaller stoops
and porticoes found in town. Their materials and textures are the
same as those seen in other neighborhoods, but here the scale and
rhythm have changed markedly.

The houses on the Point and Cliff areas provide a contrast with
the houses found in town. Their conversations are not as intimate.
Instead they are more reserved, as the houses are set back and
spaced further apart. In the winter months the structures seem
isolated from the rest of town. They are mute, and are enlivened only
during the holidays.

Summer people came from the formality of cities, and they
planned their resort architecture to be more casual, more in line with
a bathing suit than a pin-striped suit. Although these houses are
shingled and have pitched roofs, most of them are no more traditional
exclusively to Nantucket than they are to the Vineyard or the Cape,
for their forms are found in nearly every American seaside resort. At

In the Neighborhoods

the time of their construction early in this century, mass communication was beginning to bring the world closer together; even the tiny remote island received regular and timely news. Architectural styles were easily shared and copied. Some areas in America continued to develop in a provincial way, but for the most part the early decades of this century were a time of rapid and mass-produced construction.

Just after World War I, summer residents purchased the older houses on the south side of Cliff Road and renovated them, preserving their original lines. Many of these are similar to the houses in town and set on the street's edge. During the 1920s and 30s, summer residents built new mansions on the bluff side of Cliff Road. Some are very large and built in the Shingle Style; others were influenced by the Colonial Revival. They are set back far from the street, giving them forecourts that help to minimize their grand scale. The backs of the structures have sweeping verandas and terraces that reach out to the sea beyond.

Easton Street leads out to Brant Point, where a tiny lighthouse marks the shoreline. The first light was erected in 1746 and had the distinction of being the second lighthouse built in the Colonies. Over the years no fewer than ten different lighthouses have stood on this point; the present one was built in 1901. All of the previous structures were either destroyed by fire or blown down by high winds. Brant Point is a vulnerable spot. In the hours just before sunset it becomes truly special. The backlit sky casts an iridescent light on the sand and water, causing the small shells and rocks to shimmer and shine. We

The Nantucket Experience

can imagine the tall sailing ships rounding this point two centuries ago, and the whoops and shouts on board as Nantucket Town came fully into view.

Hulbert Avenue picks up at the Rotary and rounds the point. Almost all of the structures along this street date from after World War II, a time when the country was adjusting once again to prosperity and a return to the good life. They contrast in line and form with the summer mansions built along Cliff Road just after World War I. The Cliff Road mansions are tall and elegant and stately; the mansions of the 1940s and 50s, on the other hand, tend to be more horizontal and spread out. They ramble across larger lots.

Many of houses along Hulbert Avenue are also set back from the street. With few exceptions, summer residents came from cities where they had relatively little outdoor space; it was only logical that they would want green open spaces to surround their summer homes. Elaborate front and side yards developed, sometimes containing tennis courts or swimming pools. The back yards, lining the North Shore, have docks for private vessels. Hulbert Avenue terminates at Jetties Beach, one of the most popular town beaches on Nantucket.

Styles along the street range from hybrid bungalows to almost a rambling Ranch Style. None can really be ascribed one particular style—there is even one Ranch Style complete with a round Gothic tower and Greek Revival doorway. Perhaps the structures reflect the economics and confusion of the late 1940s. Because of the war effort, this was a time of vast technological advances, and when the

Regardless of age, we appreciate the special combination of space and light, water and sand, that makes a beach. On a perfect, timeless summer afternoon, not only children enjoy Jetties Beach

In the Neighborhoods

war was over, America saw one of the largest building booms in history. At this time the automobile became readily available to the majority of people, and architects planned for it in housing design. We began to see garages and carports spring up in front of homes for the first time. Driveways became more prevalent. After all, a new Ford cost $882.00 then, and gasoline was just twenty-one cents a gallon.

At the same time, radio and television were beginning to influence behavior. No longer did the family sit on the front porch in the evenings. Rather, they scrambled into the living room, and gathered around the radio to listen to "Fibber Magee and Molly" or George Burns and Gracie Allen. Soon all but the most stubborn had their own television set, or knew someone who did. Because they were no longer used, verandas disappeared from the house front, and interior living spaces became much more spacious and informal.

Actually, popular house forms haven't changed all that much since the American building boom just after World War II. The houses that have steadily appeared along Nantucket's North Shore are contemporary structures that could be built almost anywhere in the United States. Both the automobile and the television set, although greatly enhanced since World War II, are here to stay, though many of us long for the intimacy of those cool summer evenings and wide friendly verandas.

These nostalgic feelings are similar to those experienced by many Americans after the Industrial Revolution, or by the Quakers when the Lean-to house was increased to two full stories, or when the central hearth was abandoned. We will always cling to something old and comfortable before we let go and accept change, a new technology, or a new method. Advances in technology will continue to change our lives, and therefore our homes. Architecture, to be fully realized, must be accepted by the society for which it is created. Perhaps the next revolution in housing design will occur when we make yet another leap to keep up with technology. It is certain to be fraught with doubts and hesitations, but ultimately, we will change. The eternal struggle between tradition and innovation is the only thing that remains constant.

Spaces Out of Town

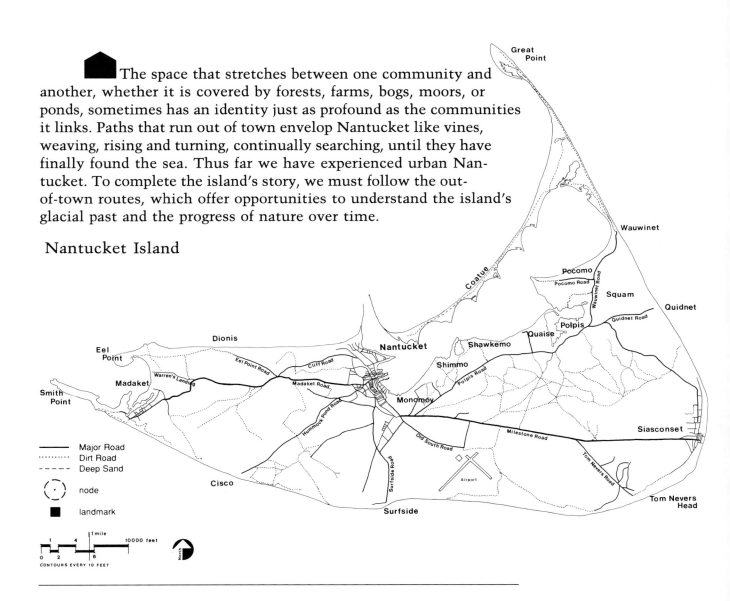

The space that stretches between one community and another, whether it is covered by forests, farms, bogs, moors, or ponds, sometimes has an identity just as profound as the communities it links. Paths that run out of town envelop Nantucket like vines, weaving, rising and turning, continually searching, until they have finally found the sea. Thus far we have experienced urban Nantucket. To complete the island's story, we must follow the out-of-town routes, which offer opportunities to understand the island's glacial past and the progress of nature over time.

Nantucket Island

Great Point

Wauwinet

Pocomo

Pocomo Road

Squam

Quidnet

Quidnet Road

Polpis

Quaise

Dionis

Nantucket

Shawkemo

Shimmo

Eel Point

Eel Point Road

Cliff Road

Polpis Road

Madaket

Warren's Landing

Madaket Road

Monomoy

Smith Point

Hummock Pond Road

Milestone Road

Siasconset

Old South Road

Airport

Tom Nevers Road

Cisco

Surfside Road

Tom Nevers Head

Surfside

—— Major Road
········· Dirt Road
- - - - Deep Sand

node

landmark

1 mile   10000 feet

North

CONTOURS EVERY 10 FEET

129

The Milestone Road to 'Sconset

The journey to 'Sconset along the Milestone Road begins at the Rotary, the vehicular node that marks the transition from somewhat urban to rural detail. This asphalt highway wasn't always here. In a different time we could have hired a coach or a box wagon and horses to transport us east to the village of 'Sconset. Passing over the deeply rutted sand paths, the wagon would creak and tilt until we were not sure of being seasick on land, or landsick at sea. Everything about going to the little fishing community on the eastern coast would have been a memorable event.

This state highway, though rather direct and unyielding, boasts some lively stories. Automobiles were not always allowed on Nantucket. Their noise frightened the horses, and at the clipping speed of twenty miles per hour, they tore up the narrow lanes in town. Clinton Folger, the mail carrier, attempted to use a touring car for mail delivery prior to their legal sanction, but the selectmen informed him that even he could not drive a car on Nantucket roads. Being an enterprising sort, the postman reasoned that the Milestone Road was a state highway and did not belong to Nantucket at all. In the early years of this century, Clinton could be seen proudly driving his car along this route to the edge of town, where he hitched his car to a pair of old horses. He sat in the driver's seat holding the reins, and much to the chagrin of the selectmen, the horses towed the car through town while Clinton delivered the mail. In the evenings he returned back to an area near the Rotary, unhitched the horses, and flew along the road, back to 'Sconset. Under pressure, the selectmen finally relented and agreed to permit automobiles in 1918.

The Milestone Road, so called because stones have been placed at each of the seven miles along its route, passes over the flattest part of the island. If we could rise above the trees, though, we could see the line of the outwash plains and valleys that were created by the glacial runoff several thousands of years ago. Along the highway our view is sharply restricted by pitch pines planted in the mid-nineteenth century. In 1912, the Nantucket State Forest was established, with over eighty thousand scotch and white pines. Although the island climate does not offer a hospitable environment for trees, the scrub oaks and pines seem to thrive in this area. In addition, nestled among the oak thickets are bayberry, sweetfern, wild indigo, huckleberries, and blueberries.

Emerging from the tunnel of trees and rising up to Bean Hill, we see an expanse of the eastern end of the island displayed over the Moors and Gibbs Pond. The water tower and the outline of 'Sconset finally come into view. To the north, over the bogs and golf course, a

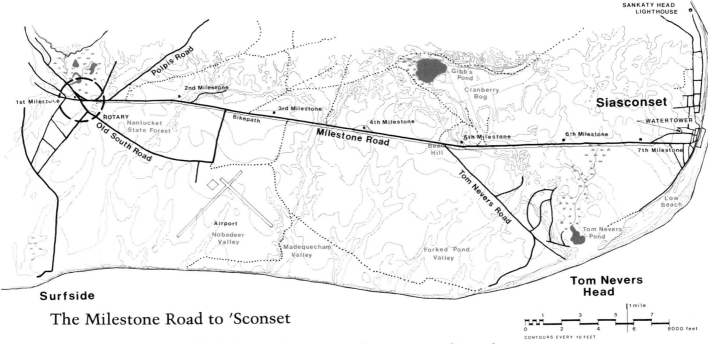

The Milestone Road to 'Sconset

red-and-white-striped lighthouse dominates the area, marking the white cliffs of Sankaty Head. The road sweeps down directly into the village, and little by little the woods diminish into a neat row of trees lining the street. If we chance to arrive in the summertime, the houses along the approach might be decorated with flowers and flags, the wide verandas will sport white wicker furniture and beach towels hung out to dry. This flurry of contemporary activity seems incongruous in this setting of modest fishing cottages built long ago, yet this coexistence of old and new promises surprise and excitement.

The mast in Post Office Square at the end of the Milestone Road catches our attention, signaling that we have arrived in Siasconset, Massachusetts. The village's full name, with its tongue twisting pronunciation, means "near the great bone" in the Indian dialect. Almost everyone uses the easier contraction of 'Sconset. The community was once a fishing station, with a few one-room shacks that dated back as far as 1680. Early in the 1800s, 'Sconset became a summer resort for Nantucketers. A visitor to the island once called it the "Newport of the Nantucketois." By the turn of the twentieth century, the picturesque village had been discovered by a number of people involved in the New York theatre circuit. Actors, writers, artists, and musicians flocked to this tiny community by the sea. The point of entry then was below the bluff on the beach, where the train station was located. Less than a hundred years ago, the scene might have been dominated by men wearing white flannels, shirts with stiff paper collars, and narrow ties, their heads shaded by Panamas

Spaces Out of Town

*Sankaty Head
Lighthouse.*

perched at rakish angles. The women, just arrived from the mainland, might have worn long, flowing dresses trimmed in ivory lace, button-up shoes, and broad-brimmed hats. They may have carried delicate parasols made in France or England. Just as colorful were the cabanas that lined the beach in front of Codfish Park.

The Nantucket Experience

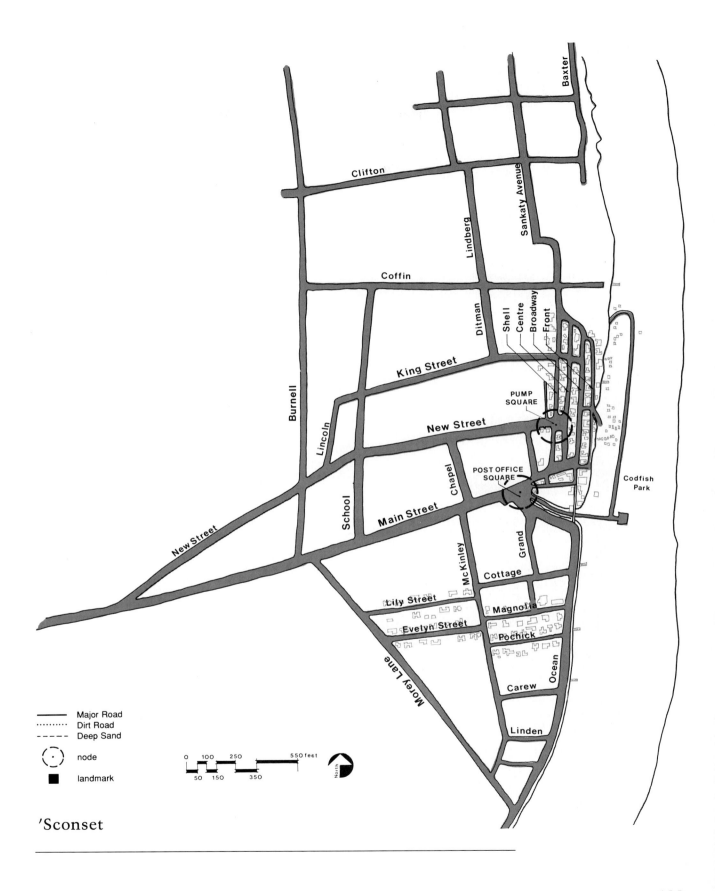

Major Road
.... Dirt Road
- - - - - Deep Sand
node
■ landmark

0   100   250   550 feet
50   150   350

North

'Sconset

Spaces Out of Town

133

'Sconset cottages and landscape have melded so well that we sometimes cannot tell where one stops and the other begins.

It became, in effect, an actor's colony during the summer months. After passing the hat around a number of times, theatre lovers raised enough money to build the Casino to house their performances. Summer theatre continued to be active until just after World War I. During the 1920s the colony began to die out as all eyes turned west once again, to the small area near Los Angeles called Hollywood. The birth of the motion picture industry caused much distress in small theatre groups across the eastern seaboard. Word got out that "talkies" would never replace the theatre, and the summer crowd at 'Sconset played on until the final act was over. The Casino is now a private tennis club, and as an unsympathetic reminder of those final days, it is also a movie theatre during the summer months.

Victorian verandas remind us of cool summer evenings, squeaky swings, and distant sounds of laughter.

The Post Office Square melts into the heart of the old village, which is edged by a small grocery and a shady colonnade. All of the lanes in the village center run to the forecourt in front of the market. Those who arrive in the village can discern little of its edges beyond the picket fences, the verandas, the porches and swings, and alternating glimpses of cottage and sea. Some of the oldest structures on Nantucket are here, many moved from an even older area near Sesachacha Pond.

We can distinguish the smaller scale of houses here compared to those seen in town. The old village, with its grass-and-sand streets and tiny fisherman's cottages, remains picturesque, exuding simplicity. Rambling roses and hollyhocks are allowed to climb up and over the architecture, creating an incredible tangle of textures. Victorian details such as spindly columns, gingerbread trim, and diamond-patterned shingles found their way to 'Sconset when the theatre crowd renovated the old structures at the turn of the twentieth century. Beginning with only one room, the little buildings sprouted ells and warts as they were needed. To soften the edges, trees and foliage were introduced in the late nineteenth century, and since then the architecture and the vegetation have become so intertwined that the animated composition of today scarcely reflects the image of a century ago.

The village center, defined by Shell, Centre, Broadway, and Front streets, was built on the very edge of the bluff, thirty feet above the water's edge. Miniature rectangular plots with narrow ways or lanes running between them define the neighborhood, and the whole experience is a wanderer's delight. Addresses are meaningless here, the houses instead boast romantic names such as "Auld Lang Syne" and "Heart's Ease."

Pump Square lies at the intersection of New and Shell streets. The well was dug during the Revolutionary War, at a cost of twenty pounds, four shillings, ninepence. For more than a hundred years villagers gathered here to wait in turn to draw their daily supply of water. It was a general meeting place for all, where gossip, news, and goods were traded, probably in that order. A modern water system took the pump's place just after the turn of the twentieth century. Its handle is now chained down and the once bustling activity has moved indoors, to the Casino, the shops, and the restaurants.

The experience of walking down Front Street with its very narrow clamshell cart tracks takes us back at least two centuries. The stark vertical facades, softened only by summer foliage, sometimes overhang the lane, and the only elements that reveal modernity are the telephone poles. The scale seems slightly smaller than human scale to us today, though it must have been appropriate for barrel carts and fishermen dragging the day's catch home. Early in the nineteenth century the 'Sconset bank was still a seawall, and toward the end of the lane we can see where the ground eroded and collapsed into the sea. We are engulfed by the view over Codfish Park and the bluff laced together by wooden staircases.

Much like the center of Nantucket Town, the surrounding neighborhoods all turn in toward the old center. We can easily see the evolution of the village by the differing styles of architecture that surround the center like the growth rings of a tree. In close proximity to the heart, on the bluffs facing the sea, are the Shingle and Stick Style homes mixed in with a few Queen Annes. As we move farther out from the center, we see a Bungalow style emerge, the same forms that can be seen from Syracuse to Los Angeles but translated in a Nantucket way. On the very edges are contemporary structures much like those found on Nantucket's north shore.

To the south of the old village is a neighborhood that confuses us. Its atmosphere would seem to make it as old as the village center, but it was actually developed during the 1880s. The builder, Edward Underhill, tried to duplicate, without precisely copying, the old village's scale and charm. Evelyn Street, named for his wife; Lily Street; and Pochick Street form this neighborhood. The houses are set back from one another further than those in the old center, making the small gravel and clamshell lanes appear wider than they really are. The streets present a scale and rhythm almost the exact opposite of Front Street. With the mixture of flowers, foliage, and open space, the

Evelyn Street in the quiet of winter.

small Underhill neighborhood is charming in a completely different way from the old center.

Perhaps no place on the island falls prey to the fickle cycles of nature more than 'Sconset. Incredibly alive with laughter, vibrant colors, and smells of barbecue and suntan oil intermingling in July and August, 'Sconset streets are reduced to silence in February. In the still of the winter months, the tiny community is indeed closed and nailed tight. Furniture is covered with white drop cloths; spotless cupboards are now bare; pictures hang crooked and unseen on the walls; a porch swing sways in the wind, its hinges groaning in protest. A lean yellow cat steals across the village square. All await the return of summer, when life can begin once again.

The Polpis Road

A Nantucket resident was once asked how one gets to 'Sconset on the Polpis Road. He gestured in that direction and replied, "You ride into the wind, up and down the hills, until you think you're gonna die, then look to the south, and there's 'Sconset."

Despite that keen observation, the Polpis Road is actually one of the most delightful pathways on the island. The surprise when we come out of the pine forest and experience the wide horizon of the rolling heath is breathtaking. Maybe the shortness of breath is, as the old gentleman described, only a result of pedaling a bicycle into the wind and up and down hills. It seems doubtful, though winds do blow hard across this expansive open area. A friend recently commented

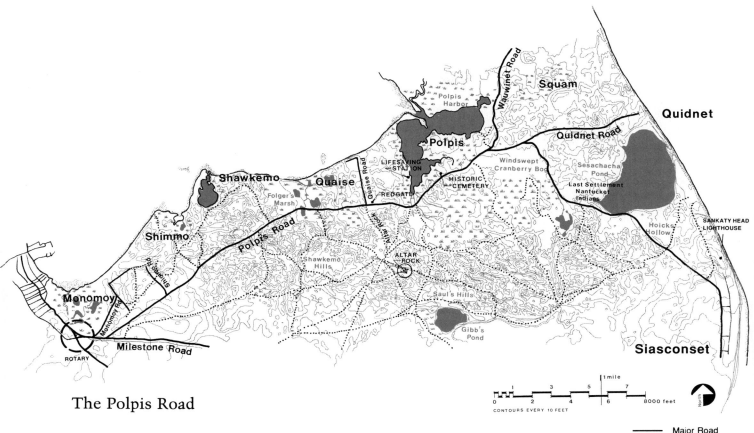

The Polpis Road

Major Road
.... Dirt Road
----- Deep Sand
node
landmark

that only on Nantucket did she have to pedal going downhill. She thought a while longer and then said with a smile, "Of course, on occasion I've also coasted uphill."

On either side of the Polpis road is a virtual choreography of nature, where heath is the predominant vegetation. On Nantucket, this expanse is commonly referred to as "the Moors." That Nantucket's moors exist at all seems a miracle, as a majority of the plant species are not found elsewhere on the American continent. Most are indigenous to the British Isles. Botanists speculate that seeds were carried to the island by ocean currents, winds, or birds. Some came nestled in the roots and soil of trees imported from Europe and the Far East. The vegetation tends to hug the ground, emphasizing the rolling landforms, and throughout the year the Moors are ablaze with natural colors. These wax and wane, only to be succeeded by a new wave of color and texture. From the violets and chickweed during the spring to the hudsonias and polygalas of June and July, to the vivid golden asters of August, and finally to the mealy plum's red berries in September and October, Nantucket's Moors provide a constant show of seasonal order and harmony.

The hills running across the upper half of the island are made up of morainal deposits and represent the farthest southward prog-

Nantucket's Moors provide a continuous display of natural color and texture.

Folger's Marsh in winter.

The old town pasture gate is now a colorful landmark on the Moors.

ress of the last glacier. Saul's Hills are the highest on the island, and the tallest point is Altar Rock, at just over one hundred feet above sea level. Along the Polpis Road is a never-ending variety of ocean views alternating with stretches of unfenced moorlands covered with wildflowers. Occasionally we see a small pond with greener, lusher foliage surrounding it. The pond's perimeter might be defined by pink marsh mallows, buttercups, and violets. Many of the most beautiful spots lie hidden among these hills and bluffs.

The Moors are scarred over by a network of deeply rutted sand paths that date back at least two hundred years. Some were originally Indian trails, and others were worn by the constant traffic to and from 'Sconset. Once a wagon—or a car, for that matter—sets out on these roads, one must follow them to the very end, for there is no turning back. Countless tales survive from the last century of wagon drivers who set out for Polpis, took a wrong turn, and found themselves and their teams going to 'Sconset whether they wanted to or not. These are still narrow, sand paths today, sometimes thickly surrounded by tall vegetation. All are only one lane wide, with few or no turnarounds. The best way to explore the Moors is on foot, stopping often to enjoy the smells and textures encountered along the way.

Just past Folger's Marsh, near the district known as Quaise, is a red gate in the fence along the road. Once the fence contained the old town pasture; now it serves as a sort of landmark sitting opposite the beginning of Altar Rock Road. From Altar Rock we can experience one of the most sweeping panoramas on the island. On a clear day in summer , after a nor'easter has swept the skies clean, we can

Spaces Out of Town

see as far as the bluffs at 'Sconset, Tom Nevers Head, Coatue, and the Great Point Lighthouse.

Polpis, in the Indian dialect, means "the divided, or branch, harbor." Although Nantucket was settled with the intention of pursuing agriculture, the mainland families soon discovered that the soil was only fit for farming in certain areas, such as Polpis. During the last century, to be from Polpis meant that you were from the country, and when the residents said of another that he was "polpisey," it meant that he was a hick, or a country boy.

The small historic cemetery adjacent to the road is possibly the only reminder of this district's age. Once this area was alive with farms and with fulling mills, which processed woolen cloth. Today we see sparse, rolling farmlands with an occasional house set directly on a hilltop. Almost all of these houses are contemporary, and their dominant siting actually diminishes nature's impact and makes the hills seem lower than they really are.

Polpis Harbor is surrounded by saltmarsh and contained by gently rising landforms on all sides. South of the harbor, nestled behind the hills, is the Hidden Forest, the largest stand of hardwoods on the island. Beech, oak, red maple, and sassafras grow in these deciduous woods. The trees are some of the tallest on the island, surviving because they were planted in a low area protected from the winds.

The path to Quidnet lies at the second fork in the Polpis Road. The district's name is a contraction of Aquidnet, meaning "at the place of the point" in the Indian dialect. Situated on the eastern shore of the island in a quarter known as Squam, this was the last settlement of the Nantucket Indians. As early as 1682 Quidnet and Sesachacha were cod-fishing and whale-sighting stations. At that time, Sesachacha Pond probably was a harbor similar to Polpis or Capaum, and like Capaum Harbor it is now closed by a sandbar. The last building at Sesachacha was taken down and moved to 'Sconset in 1820. Quidnet is now a small colony of vacation houses. Some face the Atlantic and others are oriented toward the expanse of Sesachacha Pond. All of the houses in some way reach out to the water.

At the end of the Quidnet Road is a split-rail fence that runs along the sand dunes and marks for us the path to the sea. On the other side is a floppy slotted fence, protective and yielding at the same time. Together, these edge a sand scar across the dune. They are unsuccessful barriers for the vegetation, however, as the grasses and wildflowers simply grow through them, attempting perhaps to heal over the scar.

When the sky is heavy, beset by ponderous clouds, and the wind blows over the permanently bent grasses, earth and sky merge to resemble an elaborate abstract painting. The composition is alive with every shade of blue and yellow, and the brush strokes seem to

LEFT: Polpis Harbor in summer. BELOW LEFT: The houses in Quidnet overlook Sesachacha Pond. BELOW RIGHT: Quidnet's path to the sea.

change with each new breeze. Lit from behind, the tossing plants cast continually changing shadow patterns on the path. Countless footprints disturb the sand, and we ponder how many other feet have trudged over this dune and how many eyes have encountered this expanse of darkened sea.

The Road to Surfside

Just off the Surfside Road, near the windswept head of Miacomet Pond is a thick stand of English larch and Scotch pine trees, introduced by Henry Coffin during the third quarter of the nineteenth century. As had happened on the Moors, Scotch broom and heather

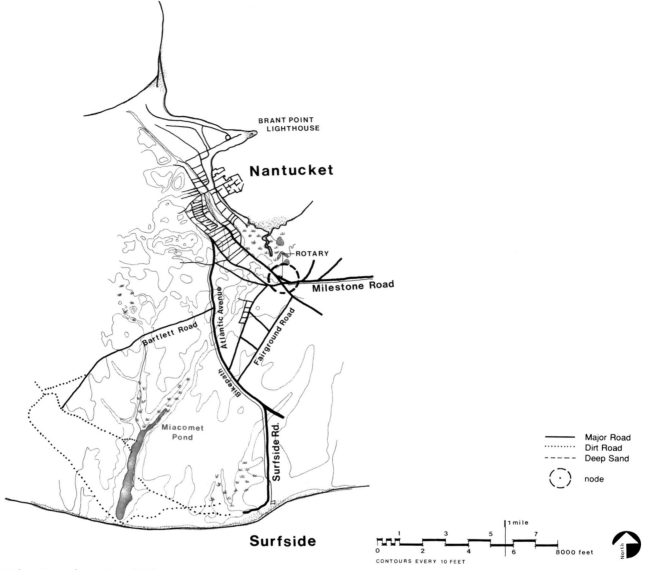

BRANT POINT
LIGHTHOUSE

Nantucket

ROTARY

Milestone Road

Atlantic Avenue

Bartlett Road

Fairground Road

Bikepath

Miacomet
Pond

Surfside Rd.

Surfside

Major Road
Dirt Road
Deep Sand

node

1 mile

0   2   4   6   8000 feet

CONTOURS EVERY 10 FEET

North

The Road to Surfside

grew up amid the pines. Over the past few years, many houses and
businesses have been built along the Surfside Road, and these
create periodic interruptions in the dense covering of trees as the
pines pull back to reveal a contemporary structure.

Surfside is a southern beach, and endless reflections from the
sun play across the water's surface. The warm and deep sand invites
us to sit and watch the rise and fall of the tide. Waves are nature's
eternal rhythms, though no two are exactly alike. Ralph Waldo Emerson was on the island in 1847 and was so taken with this expanse of
wind and water that he later recorded in his journal:

Nation of Nantucket makes its own war and peace. Place of winds, bleak, shelterless, and, when it blows, a large part of the island is suspended in the air and comes into your face and eyes as if it was glad to see you. . . .

On the seashore at Nantucket I saw the play of the Atlantic with the coast. Here was wealth: every wave reached a quarter of a mile along shore as it broke. There are no rich men, I said, to compare with these. Every wave is a fortune. One thinks of Etzlers and great projecters who will yet turn this immense waste strength to account and save the limbs of human slaves. Ah, what freedom and grace and beauty with all this might! The wind blew back the foam from the top of each billow as it rolled in, like the hair of a woman in the wind. The freedom makes the observer feel as a slave. Our expression is so slender, thin, and cramp; can we not learn here a generous eloquence?[13]

In 1873 Charles and Henry Coffin purchased a large tract of land in Surfside and attempted to develop it, complete with a full street system that marked off rectangular lots. But Surfside was not to be so easily tamed.

During the last part of the nineteenth century, speculators built a resort hotel on the bluff, and a railroad ran along Washington Street in town to the front of this hotel. Not very long after the tracks were laid, a storm covered them with sand. The rails were relaid further back from the shore. Another storm covered them again, and again they were moved back. Soon the railroad was relocated inland completely. The sea has always demanded the final word on islands, however; it took the hotel in 1899.

Surfside beach was once a grim reminder of the phrase, "Nantucket, graveyard of the Atlantic." About twenty-three miles east and forty miles south of the island lie the Nantucket shoals. In some places, only three or four feet of water cover these submerged sandbars. There have been well over five hundred shipwrecks during the island's recorded history, and most happened on the treacherous south shoals, the ones called Old Man Shoal and the Great Rip. Wreckage often washed up on the shore at Surfside. In many cases, ships would stay well out to sea and send for a Nantucket pilot to guide their craft safely through the labyrinth of shallow waters past the island. The old Nantucket Lightship, now permanently docked in the Charlestown Navy Yard, was stationed on the south shoals early in this century. It marked the steamer course to Europe and was the first object seen on the horizon by travelers to America.

By 1831 the Massachusetts Humane Society had built fourteen humane houses on Nantucket; in 1874 a United States lifesaving station was erected at Surfside. This building has Gothic Revival lines but resembles somewhat a Swiss chalet on the bluff overlooking

Surfside summer.

*Surfside
Lifesaving Station.*

the sea. The ocean gave Nantucket life, but for those who took her strength lightly, she had little patience. Even so, Man is eternally drawn to her beauty and her challenge. As we stand at the lifesaving station and look out to sea at sunset, we might grasp the true essence of a passage from Melville's *Moby Dick*:

> Why is almost every robust healthy boy with a robust healthy soul in him, at some time or other crazy to go to sea? Why upon your first voyage as a passenger, did you yourself feel such

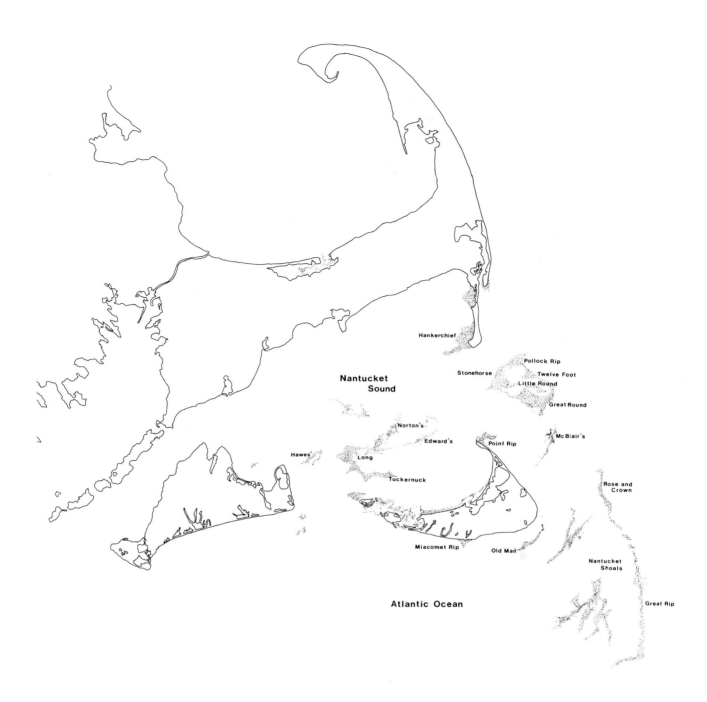

Nantucket's Shoals

Surfside

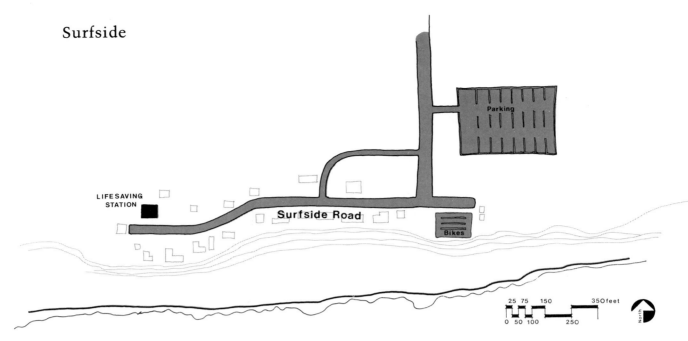

a mystical vibration, when first told that you and your ship were now out of sight of land? Why did the old Persians hold the sea holy? Why did the Greeks give it a separate deity, and own brother of Jove? Surely all this is not without meaning. And still deeper the meaning of that story of Narcissus, who because he could not grasp the tormenting, mild image he saw in the fountain, plunged into it and was drowned. But that same image we ourselves see in all rivers and oceans. It is the image of the ungraspable phantom of life: and this is the key to it all.[14]

The Road to Madaket

If we travel out of town, following Main Street west to Caton Circle, the principal street will merge with the Madaket Road. After this intersection, further down the road, we come upon the Abiah Franklin Memorial Fountain. This was set in place at the turn of the twentieth century, and meant to be a watering hole for horses. It marks the gateway to the site where the Peter Folger homestead stood in the days of the first Sherborne. The winding path leads up and over the hills to the site of the Folger farm. Pausing here, we can look over an expanse of heath and blowing grasses to the roofs of Nantucket Town beyond. Just over the hill is Maxcy's Pond. Further to the north is the black standpipe that marks the spot where the center of old Sherborne used to be.

Abiah was the youngest child of Peter and Mary Folger. She grew up on the island, leaving only to marry Josiah Franklin, of Boston. She was the elder Franklin's second wife, and not only raised her

The Roads to Madaket

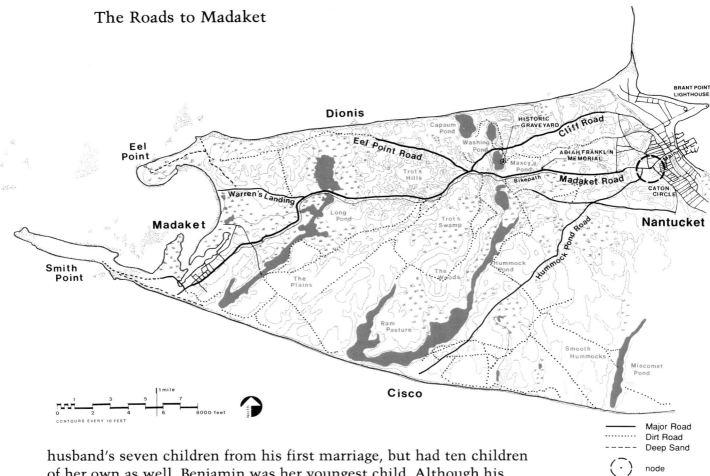

husband's seven children from his first marriage, but had ten children of her own as well. Benjamin was her youngest child. Although his mother was born on the island, we do not know whether Ben Franklin actually ever visited his relatives on Nantucket. He did write an amusing letter to his sister Jane (Mecom)[15]:

Philadelphia,
August 3, 1789

Dear Sister,

. . . I think our Family were always subject to being a little Miffy.

By the way, is our Relationship in Nantucket quite worn out? I have met with none from thence of late years, who were disposed to be acquainted with me, except Captain Timothy Foulger. They are wonderfully shy. But I admire their honest plainness of Speech. About a year ago I invited two of them to dine with me. Their answer was, that they would, if they could not do better. I suppose they did better; for I never saw them afterwards, and so had no Opportunity of showing my Miff, if I had one. . . .

Your Affectionate Brother,
B. Franklin

Spaces Out of Town

Several of Franklin's biographers have mentioned that his ingenuity and wit were acquired from his mother's side, the Nantucket branch of the Folger family.

As we proceed along the Madaket Road we will cross a large attenuated stretch of fresh water, called, appropriately, Long Pond. Many birds, most noticeably the beautiful swans, nest quietly among the reeds and marshes. Heavy stands of cattails and Queen Anne's lace dominate the pond's periphery. Long, Miacomet, and Hummock ponds are excellent examples of thin, drawn-out glacial scars that have filled with water. Some of Nantucket's former ponds are merely hollows in the landscape now, or they have become swamps, not yet completely dried up, but we can still ascertain their original outlines. The lushness of foliage in certain spots, and lighter green or bluer patches of vegetation, are telltale signs of former ponds.

The village of Madaket lies on the eastern side of Madaket Harbor. It is the westernmost community on the island. Despite the fact that the first settlers arrived here, the houses are relatively new. Many of the structures date from after 1950. Tristram's Landing, a dominant planned community to the east of Madaket Harbor, was a controversial project when it began in the 1960s. The large, identical

Madaket Harbor provides the quiet setting for these contemporary houses.

The Nantucket Experience

structures are spread out in cookie-cutter fashion, and although they are shingled, their forms and arrangement are alien to Nantucket. Rather, they display the suburban sentiment of the mainland in the late 1960s and early 70s. Madaket was formerly known as Great Neck, and the smaller, older community overlooks Hither Creek, Smith Point, and Madaket Harbor. The Hither Creek Bridge, like a giant staple, connects the community to the area of Smith Point. This vulnerable point was the traditional landing used by the Indians of Martha's Vineyard when visiting Nantucket. Over the past two hundred years, it has shifted and changed orientation and location more than any other part of Nantucket. Old maps reveal that once Smith Point was a long, narrow peninsula, and ran along the southern coast of Tuckernuck Island. Sometimes it has merged with Tuckernuck; other times, as most recently, it has become an island itself. In 1961, a hurricane washed out the Broad Creek crossing and created a small island of Smith Point. True to the sea's changing nature, Esther island was once again connected with Nantucket during a summer storm in 1986.

Cliff Road to Eel Point

If we pass out of town to the north, following the Cliff Road, we will pass by the site of the first settlement of Sherborne. Near the intersection of Cliff and Madaket roads is a tall black standpipe. This landmark stands in the area where the first Proprietors' homesteads were located. It is appropriate that, when traveling by ferry, one sees the standpipe as the first recognizable object on the north shore.

The heart of the old settlement was centered among the three ponds—Capaum, Washing, and Maxcy's. Nothing remains of the first town, however, and without the granite monument in the historic cemetery we would hardly know that it had even existed. Located on a shallow slope just east of Maxcy's Pond, the graveyard seems spare and small when we think of the splendid community that grew from the dreams and plans of those buried there. Looking out over the wild expanse of rolling hills dotted with ponds, it is hard to imagine that three hundred years ago this peaceful setting was a bustling new town.

The Eel Point Road joins the Madaket Road just past the intersection of Cliff Road. Dionis, a small beach community, is reached by this dirt path. It was named for Tristram Coffin's wife. On a clear day, standing on the high sand dunes, we can experience an extraordinary view of Coatue and Great Point to the east, and Eel Point and Tuckernuck Island to the west.

Dionis Beach.

Low tide at Eel Point reveals a swash of iridescent green.

_Taking scallops
at Eel Point._

Terns at Eel Point.

Spaces Out of Town

The road terminates at Eel Point. It was near here, around Warren's Landing, that Thomas Macy, Edward Starbuck, and Isaac Coleman spent their first winter on Nantucket. Even in 1659, this sparse dune environment could not have possibly supplied much shelter. The wind-shaped dunes are constantly shifting, and only the hardy beach grass can withstand this changing environment. In fact, it is the beach grass that helps to stabilize the dunes. Eel point was not formed by the glaciers as was the central body of Nantucket. Instead, the tidal flats are the product of the wind- and tide-carried sediments. Tire tracks and heavy traffic upset the precarious natural balance in this fragile area. Terns have established their nesting grounds on Eel Point, and it is fitting that their piercing cries are the only animate sounds heard over the roar of wind and waves.

Wauwinet, Great Point, and Coatue

Located at the head of Great Harbor, Wauwinet is the gateway to Coatue, Coskata, and Great Point. Its name is that of the Indian sachem who ruled over this section of the island. The tiny community of vacation cottages clusters around the large mass of the old Wauwinet Hotel. Unique in its setting, with harbor on one side and ocean on the other, Wauwinet has been an attractive summer resort for the past thirty years. A private dirt road bisects the peninsula.[16] It bumps and rolls and curves with the land, becoming more and more sandy until it is only deep sand. From that point on, a four-wheel-drive vehicle or sturdy legs are necessary to continue.

Just past Wauwinet is the narrowest part of this long, graceful arm, called the Haulover. It acquired the name because fishermen used to carry their small boats over this spot rather than go around Great Point. The arm was opened during a nor'easter on December 15, 1896, and the harbor and ocean were joined. Illustrating the fickle nature of the sea, the gap closed again twelve years later.

Coatue means "at the pine woods" in the Indian dialect. This region is a long and delicate sandbar that has been masterfully scalloped on the harbor side by tidal currents. These currents alternate up and down the coast, piling sand first in one direction, then the other. The six points of Coatue are the most ecologically fragile and scenically vulnerable area on Nantucket. A deep sand road with low vegetation on either side proceeds along the bar. Traveling this path, we can observe the skeletal remains of slat fences that used to hold the shifting sand back from the road. Now—bent, twisted, and rusting—they only scar the landscape.

Perhaps a half-dozen cottages have been built on this bar. They represent the barest indication that humans were even here.

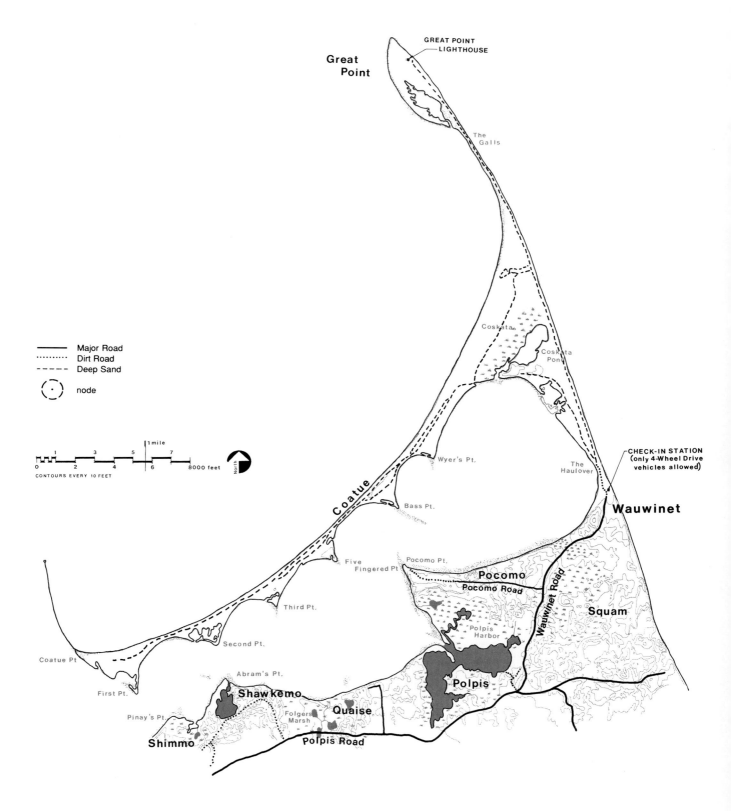

Legend

———	Major Road
·········	Dirt Road
– – –	Deep Sand
⊙	node

CONTOURS EVERY 10 FEET

North

GREAT POINT LIGHTHOUSE

Great Point

The Galls

Coskata

Coskata Pond

Coatue

Wyer's Pt.

CHECK-IN STATION (only 4-Wheel Drive vehicles allowed)

The Haulover

Wauwinet

Bass Pt.

Five Fingered Pt.

Pocomo Pt.

Pocomo

Pocomo Road

Wauwinet Road

Squam

Third Pt.

Polpis Harbor

Second Pt.

Coatue Pt.

Abram's Pt.

First Pt.

Shawkemo

Polpis

Pinay's Pt.

Folgers Marsh

Quaise

Shimmo

Polpis Road

Wauwinet, Great Point, and Coatue

Spaces Out of Town

155

The Nantucket Experience

Coatue in winter.

A lone Lean-to stands inland. The shifting landscape has already started to crawl up the shingled walls and reclaim the house—a demonstration that eventually nature will emerge the victor. The flat winter landscape, with its blond grasses fluid in the wind, is punctuated only by this one lonely Lean-to. In its stark simplicity, the whole composition resembles a quiet moment in an Andrew Wyeth painting.

Alternating glimpses of dunes and water dominate the scene until we finally arrive at Coatue Point, where all of Nantucket Town is revealed across the water.

Just ten miles separate Great Point from Monomoy Island on the southeast end of Cape Cod. This is a shoreline landscape bounded by the Great Harbor, Nantucket Sound, and the Atlantic Ocean. Shallow sand dunes, linear sloping beaches, marshes, and vegetation blend into one another, and are home to many small mammals, birds, and fish. Osprey have their own protected breeding grounds here. Indeed, Great Point belongs to them, not really to humans at all. We are only visitors here, and should walk softly.

A white lighthouse marks the end of the point. Great Point's first lighthouse was a frame structure built in 1784. It stood until

Spaces Out of Town

November 1816, when it was destroyed by fire. Two years later a second one was built, this time of stone. In the early decades of this century it stood about a quarter of a mile from the end of the point. Over the years the ocean has carved away at this coastline, and during a winter storm in 1984 the stone lighthouse toppled into the sea. The light that stands today was built as an exact replica of the second one and dedicated in the summer of 1986. This time, however, it was situated considerably further inland and anchored many feet below the surface of the ground. The eerie-looking ruins of the 1818 lighthouse, the foundations at least, remain, but they will not be here for much longer. Soon they, too, will succumb to the sea. It is in the ruins of that manmade structure that we can visualize the power of the sea and the ultimate vulnerability of humankind. The old lighthouse, like many others, will soon be only in the memories of a special few. Standing on Great Point, so close to town and yet so far away from civilization, we might easily ponder the meaning of islands, and question how Nantucket came to be.

The out-of-town journeys are different from those experienced in Nantucket Town because outside the urban fabric, nature is the principal protagonist in Nantucket's play. In town, on the other hand, nature has only a supporting role as architecture assumes the lead. We can never take all the journeys possible on the island, for each of us composes his or her own travels in time based on memories from childhood and from past Nantucket visits. Furthermore, the journeys often change as our lives and Nantucket change. Perhaps the next journey should be the one that you create for yourself.

Memorable journeys are a series of vignettes laced together by time, with no real beginning or ending. They can be found almost anywhere, not only on Nantucket. Look for a place with at least a few old buildings—the more the better—and use a little imagination. Be critical but understanding of the buildings as you try to ascertain their rhythm and their scale. Notice their texture and color. Check for contradictions in the context. Ask yourself if a building is truly representative of the society that created it. If it is not, consider what happened. If it is, then you are allowed an even more profound understanding of that society. When you visit a new community, you can focus your perceptions the same as for a historic one. Determine whether its neighborhoods are easily identified. Are the landmarks helpful as wayfinders? Can you find the gateways? Moreover, do the buildings *sing* and are the rhythm and harmony of a neighborhood in sync with the town's history and setting? Seek out the oldest areas in a town, the quietest as well as the busiest, and see if the doorknobs speak to you.

Although costumes and context may change, familiar faces and landscapes are everywhere—familiar because they are part of the American story we all carry within ourselves. The images might be of a young Confederate soldier, home after the War Between the States, surveying what is left of the farm; a family of eight who sold everything to head west to San Francisco and the Gold Rush of '49; a Vermont Green Mountain Boy; the smell of Creole cooking; the roar of Manhattan—wherever images are made in space and time. In the vast American landscape there are endless theatre sets, waiting for actors to play on them.

Along the Madaket Road, 1982. Development began in this area shortly after this photograph was taken. The wide expanse of wild flowers is now dotted with large houses.

Afterword

The evolution of Nantucket Town is in many ways similar to that of numerous historic New England towns. Once highly prosperous, they later suffered as a result of western expansion and a depressed economy. This dormant period was followed by a second burst of wealth that helped to pay for the preservation and renovation of the community. Unlike many communities, however, where only a very select few of the more outstanding examples have been preserved, Nantucket boasts over eight hundred historic buildings. Not only the houses of the wealthy, but also the dwellings of the tradesmen, the schoolteachers, and the shopkeepers have been left for us. It is a happy coincidence that the same remoteness that impeded the advancement of island architecture also allowed it to be preserved.

Today several agencies and commissions work very hard to keep the island's history and architecture from quickly disappearing under a flood of new development. With real estate values escalating at nearly 20 percent a year on the island, the race between speculators and conservation groups is indeed on. In 1970 the Historic District Commission (HDC) was established. This body maintains architectural standards and acts as a design review board for the town. They have published guidelines for building on Nantucket, and all applications for new construction and modification must first pass their careful review. As a designer and an educator, rigorous design restrictions have always distressed me; however, the alternative is unthinkable here. Consider for a moment the unchecked development that has occurred on Martha's Vineyard, or the Hamptons, or, for that matter, at any ocean community on the eastern and western seaboards. That the old town of Nantucket has retained its historic charm and scale should be largely credited to this agency.

Summer tourists arrive hourly to enjoy Nantucket's fresh ocean breezes, the nostalgic charm of the villages, and the colorful expanse of the Moors.

Because of the Nantucket Conservation Foundation, about 25 percent of the island will be left in a natural state. Established as a nonprofit organization in 1963, the foundation is sustained by voluntary donations from its many members. In addition to preserving large tracts of open land, it does much to foster education and research. It sponsors seminars and classes, and provides grants for the study of the island's many ecosystems. Through donations, the Nantucket Conservation Foundation holds properties as diverse as moors, forests, ponds, and bogs, and each tract is marked by a maroon roadside post topped by the foundation's distinctive logo. Their latest large acquisitions were the Moors area surrounding Altar Rock and the Sanford Farm on the Madaket Road. Every year the foundation publishes a map of its holdings, available for a nominal fee at their office at 118 Cliff Road. Many of the holdings of the Nantucket Conservation Foundation are open to the public. (As with other conservation lands in the United States, visitor access is a privilege. It is our responsibility to see that we leave these areas clean and unspoiled for the enjoyment of others.)

One of the most controversial methods for land preservation in the United States happened in 1983 with the founding of the Nantucket Land Bank. With land costs continually rising, something had to be done before all of the land on the island was priced out of the market for public use. The town voted to enact a 2 percent transfer fee for all real estate transactions on the island. The buyer pays the tax. All of the proceeds will be used by the Land Bank Commission to acquire open space, and the goal is to purchase 15 percent of the island. These lands will be left in the natural state, and for the most part used for public recreation. More than 700 acres have been acquired in this way, including beach fronts, ponds and moors.

So much of the historic preservation and the still-open land must be attributed to the endeavors of the various Nantucket commissions. Most contemporary development is done by a multi-faceted group of people not bound by any island traditions; therefore they build sometimes in isolation, without regard for the impact on the surrounding areas. Centuries ago a strong Quaker hold required people to build for the common good of the community, and whaling prosperity allowed individuals to give something back to the community that had helped to produce the wealth. The thousands of trees, the sidewalks and squares stand as reminders of this generosity. There is no common thread today, so we must have regulatory boards to do the work that the overseers of the Society used to do.

Nantucket can only be experienced over time, and just as time clicks away, the environment must respond to the changing needs, and sometimes whims, of the people who live there. The age-old question of innovative development or traditional development has always been a problem on the tiny island. The first upset in the Quaker's lives was the raising of the Typical house to two full stories, front and back; this was followed by the European Classical influence, a style distinctly imported, not evolved; then came the Romantic era, with its resort architecture—again imported, not local to the island. This very diversity of architectural styles, however, has produced the exciting and sometimes humorous conversations we can sense among the old buildings in town.

Despite stylistic differences, most of the architecture up to and including the Romantic era had one thing in common: the community was considered foremost, not the individual. Diversity in architecture was brought together not by sameness, but by a common spirit. Today we live in a pluralist society with more choices than our forefathers ever thought possible. Different kinds of people use and enjoy the island in different ways. For the residents, Nantucket is home. For others, Nantucket is their summer home, and still more of us journey there for a day, or a week, to find our home in time. Speculators see Nantucket not as home in any context, but as a temporary place to stop on their way to someplace else.

For generations there has been a peaceful coexistence of old and new architecture on Nantucket. This relationship might not continue, however, for it is difficult to blend with an environment that is so rich in history and vision. The simple truth is that new development will require time to evoke the same historic images that the old town has because new development, even following the local vernacular trend, has no history itself to speak of. And even though the new houses have pitched roofs and are covered with shingles, they are speechless. Like children not yet able to talk, they must find their own meanings in life.

The old buildings are three-dimensional reminders of great-great-grandparents; they are events, and they are representations of real human experience. Just as an infant cannot compete with an adult for depth of character and interest, neither can a new structure call forth the same images as an old one. On occasion, though, I have met children who are wise beyond their years or adults content to remain only twelve. Architecture, too, can cross this age gap. The question is not one of building a structure that meets Commission criteria and matches old styles, but a more complex one—of achieving a meaning just as evocative as those which preceded it, for meaning is the invisible structural glue that holds everything together.

How do you evoke meaning in a new piece of architecture? Tough question. Perhaps you start first with a little sympathy and respect for what has happened before, then follow this with an education into the motivations that produced the images. Nantucket is not like the mainland; it is unique and cannot be compromised or compared. Everything (including new construction) built on the island today should be approached as a remodel, as anything new in the environment is in reality a remodel of the older environment. New buildings can speak to the old ones in dialogues just as profound as those sensed among the old buildings in town, though the communication is more difficult. The dialogue becomes more like conversations that transcend vast age gaps. The burden falls on the designers of the newer structures to be more sympathetic and understanding of the old.

New development should include exterior spaces that encourage individuals to gather rather than remain in isolation, that encourage exploration and discovery. It needs to be varied and adventuresome, and of course, speak softly to nature. It is important that human scale be continued in the new construction, and even though a structure's harmony may change, the rhythm must remain the same. New streets should not be long and straight like the mainland's subdivisions, but rather like the memorable streets in town, which roll and curve with the topography. The natural landscape should be disturbed as little as possible.

The year-round population on the island is now hovering at about seventy-five hundred. During the summer this increases to forty thousand. Because of rising costs, the butcher, the baker, and the candlestick maker have been priced out of the market. A community in the true sense of the word cannot exist without its basic services—the shops and markets—or at least it can't exist for very long. The city center has become gentrified with luxury shops open in the summer months; it remains nearly a ghost town in the winter.

"We can never take all the journeys possible on the island. . . ."

Afterword

There is talk of increasing the 2 percent transfer fee on real estate to 2.5 percent. The extra half percent would go into a fund for affordable housing. Perhaps this is a step in the right direction. Centuries ago, the original Proprietors offered half-shares in the corporation to craftsmen willing to come to the island to practice their trades. Maybe this old concept has some application yet.

My musings cannot be seen as naive suggestions, but rather as suggestions that will, I hope, initiate discussions and creative research to solve the unique problems facing Nantucket today. In days gone by, these problems might have been solved on a front stoop, or over coffee, or at Town Meeting. Today, only economics can offer possible solutions, in the form of state and local tax breaks, revenue bonds, and subsidies. If Nantucket is to stay the way we would all like it to be, the growth problems must be solved soon, and with ample community involvement and input. This is an enormous challenge set before the community planners, for if Nantucket can solve these problems, the results might serve as a role model for other historic and seaside communities in America.

We do seem to prefer a complex environment rather than one that is designed for us right down to the color of the doorknobs. Despite extended families and journeys in time, though, most of us live in an isolated present. Gone are the communal roots of the past. Change is inevitable, and our task is not really to stop change, because we can't. Perhaps our purpose should be simply to guide it.

The simple fact remains that this small bit of land is fragile. Once gone, it is nonrenewable, as are the delightful and surprising views and the unique interplay of architecture, nature, and sea that we glimpse from time to time. Once those experiences are gone, like the land, they are gone forever, and no degree of "planned spontaneity" will ever bring them back again. The original proprietors were wise in trying to keep the majority of the island wild, for Nantucket must never be completely tamed.

As I stated in the beginning of these journeys, a significant element of the Nantucket experience occurs after you have returned to America. It happens usually in the off-season, when you are thinking of something else. You reach into the pocket of a favorite jacket and pull out a handful of sand and shells, or pieces of a well-worn map. A smile escapes and broadens as the fragments dance before your eyes and transform into a special, personal image of the little island far out to sea.

Notes

1. Bradford Torrey, ed., *The Writings of Henry David Thoreau*, Journal Number 7, 1906, p. 93-94.

2. Some historians have speculated that the word Bocochico is of Spanish origin and means "little river." Before the tract east of Federal was created, a small stream ran through the area.

3. In 1846 there were two very competitive volunteer firefighting teams. It was mutually agreed that whichever team arrived on the scene first would have the honor of holding the hose and putting out the blaze. On that night in July, both the Cataract No. 6 and the Fountain No. 8 arrived at the same time. The volunteers began to argue about who would put out the fire; meanwhile the blaze spread rapidly and soon was hopelessly out of control.

4. The Nantucket Historical Association maintains several historic houses that can be visited for a nominal fee. They include: The Oldest House, on Sunset Hill; the Nathanial Macy House, Liberty Street; the 1800 House, Mill Street; the Greater Light, Howard Street; and the Hadwen-Satler House, at 96 Main Street. Recently, the splendid Federal House at 99 Main Street was bequeathed to the Association, and it, too, might soon be open for visits.

5. Kevin Lynch dedicated his life to the concept of environmental imageability. It was in his book, *The Image of a City*, that he introduced and explored the ideas of *district, edge, node, path,* and *landmark*. To his original list I have suggested two others: *gateway* and *physical events*.

6. There were five mills in operation on Nantucket at one time. The Roundtop Mill stood on the site of the New North Cemetery, and four other mills were located on the hills to the west of town. The Spider Mill stood on what is now Prospect Hill Cemetery; the Charles Bunker Mill stood on Chicken Hill to the east; Brimstone Mill to the east of Chicken Hill; and the sole survivor, the Charles Swain Mill, east of the Brimstone Mill.

7. The English spelling of the name was Foulger, but the family changed the spelling to Folger when they moved to America. When they later donated the building for the museum, they specified that the old spelling of the name be used.

8. Harriet Barnes Thayer, "Hereditary Architecture," *Proceedings of the Nantucket Historical Association*, 1919, p. 49–50.

9. Harriet Barnes Thayer, "Hereditary Architecture," (see note 8).

10. I am grateful to Mr. Fred Cook for calling my attention to this construction and showing me the attic of the Church.

11. There is evidence that the house originally had twin dormers in the front facade. When it was restored in 1928–29 the new owner decided to omit them.

12. In October 1987 the house was struck by lightning. The unique chimney and part of the roof were destroyed. At the time of this writing, many volunteers are working to repair the damage so that the house may soon be open again to visitors.

13. Merton M. Sealts, Jr., ed., *The Journals and Miscellaneous Notebooks of Ralph Waldo Emerson*, p. 62–63.

14. Herman Melville, *Moby Dick*, 1851. New American Library version, p. 23.

15. Albert Henry Smyth, *The Writings of Benjamin Franklin*, vol. X, p. 33.

16. Before proceeding along this private road, one must stop at the check-in station and register. Only four-wheel-drive vehicles equipped with a shovel and a tow rope are allowed to pass. Visitors without four-wheel-drive transportation may walk in, however. As you wander further out on the point, you will realize why the heavy-duty jeeps and trucks are required: the sand is very deep, and even the locals sometimes get stuck.

Bibliography

Albertson, Alice O. *Nantucket Wildflowers.* New York: G.P. Putnam's Sons, 1921.

Andrews, Wayne. *Architecture in New England.* Brattleboro, Vt.: The Stephen Greene Press, 1973.

———. *Architecture, Ambition, and Americans.* New York: The Free Press, 1964.

Bachelard, Gaston. *The Politics of Space.* Translated by Maria Jolas. Boston: Beacon Press, 1964.

Balliett, Blue. *The Ghosts of Nantucket.* Camden, Me.: Down East Books, 1984.

Burroughs, Polly. *Guide to Nantucket.* 3rd rev. ed. Boston: Globe Pequot Press, 1984.

Calvino, Italo. *Invisible Cities.* Translated by William Weaver. New York: Harcourt, Brace, Jovanovich, 1974.

Chamberlain, Barbara Blau. *These Fragile Outposts.* Garden City, N.Y.: The Natural History Press, 1964.

Ching, Francis D.K. *Architecture: Form, Space and Order.* New York: Van Nostrand, Reinhold Co., 1979.

Chisholm, Christopher; Holzheimer, Robert; Robinson, John. *Nantucket Island: An Analysis of the Natural and Visual Resources.* Cambridge, Mass.: Harvard Graduate School of Design, Dept. of Landscape Architecture, 1974.

Coffin, Marie, comp. *The History of Nantucket: A Bibliography of Source Material with Index and Inventory.* Nantucket: Nantucket Historical Trust, 1970.

Crosby, Everett U. *Ninety-Five Per Cent Perfect.* Nantucket: Inquirer & Mirror, 1944.

———. *Nantucket in Print.* Nantucket: Tetaukimmo Press 1946.

Cullen, Gordon. *Townscape.* London: The Architectural Press, 1961.

Cummings, Abbott Lowell. *The Framed Houses of Massachusetts Bay, 1625–1725.* Cambridge, Mass.: Harvard Univ. Press, 1979.

De Crevecoeur, J. Hector St. John. *Letters from an American Farmer*. New York: Penguin Books, 1981. (Originally published 1782.)

Douglas-Lithgow, R.A. *Nantucket: A History*. New York: G.P. Putnam and Sons, 1914.

Duprey, Kenneth. *Old Houses on Nantucket*. New York: Hastings House, 1984.

Eberlein, Harold D. and Hubbard, Cortlandt V. *American Georgian Architecture*. London: Pleiades Books, 1952.

Forman, Henry Chandlee. *Early Nantucket and Its Whale Houses*. New York: Hastings House, 1966.

Fowlkes, George Allen. *A Mirror of Nantucket: An Architectural History of the Island, 1686–1850*. Plainfield, N.J.: Press of Interstate, 1959.

Gardner, Will. *The Coffin Saga*. Cambridge, Mass.: Riverside Press, 1949.

Giedion, Sigfried. *Space, Time, and Architecture*. 3rd ed. Cambridge, Mass.: Harvard Univ. Press, 1954.

Godfrey, Edward K. *The Island of Nantucket, What It Was and What It Is*. Boston: Lee & Shepard, 1882.

Greene, Herb. *Mind and Image, An Essay on Art and Architecture*. Lexington, Ky.: Univ. Press of Kentucky, 1976.

Hall, Edward T. *The Hidden Dimension*. 1st ed. Garden City, N.Y.: Doubleday & Co., 1966.

———. *The Silent Language*. Garden City, N.Y.: Doubleday & Co., 1959.

Hamlin, Talbot. "Nantucket." *Architectural Review*. August 1947, pp. 54–57.

Hare, Lloyd C. M. *The Greatest American Woman, Lucretia Mott*. New York: American Historical Society, 1937.

Hinchman, Lydia S. *Early Settlers of Nantucket*. Rutland, Vt.: Charles E. Tuttle Co., 1980.

Hoyt, Edwin P. *The Life of an Island*. Brattleboro, Vt.: Stephen Greene Press, 1980.

Jacobs, Jane. *The Death and Life of Great American Cities*. New York: Vintage Books, 1961.

Kimball, Fiske. *Domestic Architecture of the American Colonies and of the Early Republic*. Mineola, N.Y.: Dover Publications, 1966.

Klein, William R. "Nantucket Tithes for Open Space." *Planning* 52 (August 1986) 10–13.

Krier, Rob. *Urban Space*. New York: Rizzoli International, 1979.

———. *Elements of Architecture*. Architectural Design Profile. New York: St. Martin's Press, 1983.

Lancaster, Clay. *The Architecture of Historic Nantucket*. New York: McGraw-Hill, 1972.

Lang, J. Christopher. *Building with Nantucket in Mind*. Nantucket: Nantucket Historic District Commission, 1978.

Lynch, Kevin. *The Image of the City*. Cambridge, Mass.: MIT Press, 1960.

———. *What Time Is This Place?* Cambridge, Mass.: MIT Press, 1972.

Bibliography

McCalley, John. *Nantucket Yesterday and Today*. Mineola, N.Y.: Dover, 1981.

Macy, Obed. *The History of Nantucket*. Clifton, N.J.: Augustus M. Kelley, 1972. (Originally published 1835 and 1880.)

Macy, William F. *The Story of Old Nantucket*. Nantucket: Inquirer & Mirror, 1983. (Originally published 1915.)

———. *The Nantucket Scrap Basket*. Boston: Houghton Mifflin Co., 1916.

Melville, Herman. *Moby Dick*. New York: New American Library, 1961. (Originally Harper and Bros., 1851.)

Moore, Charles, and Bloomer, Kent C. *Body, Memory and Architecture*. New Haven: Yale Univ. Press, 1977.

Moore, Charles, and Allen, Gerald. *Dimensions*. New York: Architectural Record Books, 1976.

Moore, Charles; Allen, Gerald; and Lyndon, Donlyn. *The Place of Houses*. New York: Holt, Rinehart & Winston, 1974.

Mumford, Lewis. *Sticks and Stones*. Mineola, N.Y.: Dover Publications, 1924 and 1955.

Noble, Allen G. *Wood, Brick, and Stone*, Amherst: Univ. of Massachusetts Press, 1984.

Passini, Romedi. *Wayfinding in Architecture*. New York: Van Nostrand Reinhold Co., 1984.

Piaget, Jean. *The Child's Conception of the World*. Translated by Joan and Andrew Tomlinson. Totowa, N.J.: Littlefield, Adams, 1972.

Porter, Tom. *How Architects Visualize*. New York: Van Nostrand Reinhold Co., 1979.

Rapoport, Amos, and Kantor, Robert E. "Complexity and Ambiguity in Environmental Design." *Journal of the American Institute of Planners* 33 (July 1967) 210–21.

Rasmussen, Steen Eiler. *Experiencing Architecture*. 2nd U.S. ed. Cambridge, Mass.: MIT Press, 1962.

Rice, Mabel Agnes. *Trees and Shrubs of Nantucket*. Ann Arbor, Mich.: Edwards Bros., Inc., 1946.

Robinson, J.H. *Guide to Nantucket*. 1948.

Rudofsky, Bernard. *Streets for People*. Garden City, N.Y.: Doubleday, 1969.

Sansom, Joseph, Esq. "Nantucket," *The Portfolio* 5. Philadelphia, 1811.

Scott, Geoffrey. *The Architecture of Humanism*. 2nd ed. Garden City, N.Y.: Doubleday, 1954.

Scully, Vincent, Jr. *The Shingle Style Today*. New York: George Braziller, 1974.

Sealts, Merton M. Jr., ed. *The Journals and Miscellaneous Notebooks of Ralph Waldo Emerson*, vol. 10. Cambridge, Mass.: Harvard Univ. Press, 1973.

Sinclair, Peg B. *Victorious Victorians*. New York: Holt, Rinehart and Winston, 1985.

Smyth, Albert Henry. *The Writings of Benjamin Franklin*, vols. 1–10. New York: Macmillan Co. 1907.

Sommer, Robert. *Personal Space.* Englewood Cliffs, N.J.: Prentice-Hall, 1969.

Stackpole, Edouard A. *Rambling Through the Streets and Lanes of Nantucket.* New Bedford, Mass.: Reynolds-DeWalt Printing, Inc., 1951.

———. "The Great Fire of 1846." *Proceedings of the Nantucket Historical Association.* 1946.

———. "The History of Nantucket." Lecture at the Whaling Museum, September 10, 1986.

Starbuck, Alexander. *The History of Nantucket: County, Island, and Town.* C.E. Tuttle, 1969.

Sterling, Dorothy. *The Outer Lands: A Natural History Guide to Cape Cod, Martha's Vineyard, Nantucket, Block Island, & Long Island.* New York: W.W. Norton, 1978.

Stevens, William O. *Old Nantucket: The Far-Away Island.* New York: Dodd, Mead and Co., 1936.

Thayer, Harriet Barnes, "Hereditary Architecture." *Proceedings of the Nantucket Historical Association.* 1919, pp. 46–50.

Torrey, Bradford, ed. *The Writings of Henry David Thoreau.* New York: AMS Press, 1968.

Tuan, Yi-Fu. *Topophilia: A Study of Environmental Perception, Attitudes, and Values.* Englewood Cliffs, NJ: Prentice-Hall, Inc., 1974.

Venturi, Robert. *Complexity and Contradiction in Architecture.* New York: Museum of Modern Art, 1966.

Vineyard Open Land Foundation. *Looking at the Vineyard.* 1973.

Whiffen, Marcus, and Koeper, Frederick. *American Architecture 1607–1976.* Cambridge, Mass.: MIT Press, 1981.

Wittkower, Rudolf. *Architectural Principles in the Age of Humanism.* 2nd ed. London: A. Tiranti, 1952.

Worth, Henry B. "Nantucket Lands and Landowners." *Bulletin of the Nantucket Historical Association* 2, nos. 1 & 7, 1928.

———. "House Lots of Settlers." *Bulletin of the Nantucket Historical Association* 2, no. 2, 1928.

———. "Original Layouts on the Harbor." *Bulletin of the Nantucket Historical Association* 2, no. 4, 1928.

———. "Nantucket Streets." *Bulletin of the Nantucket Historical Association* 2. no. 5, 1928.

Map References Used for This Book

Many of the maps were graciously provided by the Research Library of the Peter Foulger Museum.

Proprietors' Record Book:

    Plat no. 1, folio 8, Wescoe Acre Lots, 1712

        folio 37, West Monomoy Lots, Fishlots, Bocochico

        folio 151, Water Lots around the Wharves, 1774

        folio 224, The Amendments, 1804

        folio 224, North Beach Shares, 1805

    Plat No. 2, Brant Point and Meadows, 1803

Town of Nantucket, 1834. William Coffin, Jr.

Nantucket Harbor, 1848. A.D. Bache, U.S. Coast Survey, Library of Congress, Map Division.

Town of Nantucket, 1858. H.F. Walling, Library of Congress, Map Division.

The Historical Map of the Island of Nantucket, 1869. The Rev. F.C. Ewer, D.D.

The Island of Nantucket, 1874. The Rev. F.C. Ewer, D.D.

Bird's Eye View of the Town of Nantucket, 1881. William O. Lincoln

New Map of the Streets of Nantucket, 1882. E.K. Godfrey

Village of Siasconset, 1888. Harry Platt, Publisher: E.T. Underhill and Co.

Layout of Wharf Area, 1895. W.F. Codd

Siasconset, Massachusetts, 1905. J.H. Robinson

Map of that Section of the Town of Nantucket which was Destroyed by the Fire, 1907. S.H. Jenks, Jr.

Town of Nantucket Survey, 1967. Sherburne Associates

Original Layouts on the Harbor, 1969. From Alexander Starbuck, The History of Nantucket: Island, County and Town.

House Lot Selection, 1665--680, 1969. From Alexander Starbuck, *The History of Nantucket: Island, County and Town.*

The Town and County of Nantucket, 1975. Schofield Brothers, Inc.

Nantucket Official Zoning Map, 1975. James Elder, Jr.

United States Geological Survey (USGS), 1975. (4 maps) Department of the Interior

Nantucket Official Zoning Map, 1979.

Nantucket Official Zoning Map, 1980.

Properties of the Nantucket Conservation Foundation, 1986. Nantucket Conservation Foundation.

Massachusetts. Rand McNally.

About the Author

Catherine Garland lives in California—in an old house by California standards (forty years)—but, she says, her spiritual home is in New England. "It is the sense of history that keeps calling me back. The heritage that has been handed down from my immigrant grandparents is one of exploring new places and seeking to understand them. The contradiction of the old and the new—and the peaceful coexistence of the two—attracts me."

Ms. Garland's architectural firm, Design Principles, specializes in adaptive reuse of residential and small commercial buildings. She also teaches design and architecture at California Polytechnic, Pomona, where in 1986 she was presented with the Meritorious Performance and Professional Promise Award for excellence in teaching. She holds a B.A. degree in Art History from the University of California at Irvine, and a B.S. in Architecture from California Polytechnic, Pomona.

When she came back to Cal Poly in 1984, Ms. Garland was asked to teach an architecture class for non-majors, called "The Meaning of Architecture," and after teaching that course several years, she became intrigued by the idea that many adults seem to have lost the ability to see or understand their built environment. "It then occured to me that some environments were far more memorable than others, and I began to research the criteria for 'memorable environments.' This book represents my own quest to understand completely how and why the spaces of Nantucket are so memorable."